B"H

BAAL SHEM TOV

RABBI YISRAEL BEN ELIEZER
THE LEGENDARY KABBALAH MASTER

DEUTERONOMY

MYSTICAL STORIES ON
THE WEEKLY TORAH PORTION

VOLUME V

Compiled and Freely Adapted
By **Tzvi Meir Cohn**

BST Publishing
Cleveland, Ohio

First Printing 2011
Collection, adaptation, introductory material by Tzvi Meir Cohn
© 2011 by Tzvi Meir Cohn
Printed in the United States of America

To receive the Baal Shem Tov Times, a Free weekly newsletter, register at our website, www.baalshemtov.com.

For information regarding permission to reprint material from this book, please e-mail your request to info@bstpublishing.com

Library of Congress Control Number: 2011914217
Library of Congress subject heading:
1. Hasidim — Legends. 2. Baal Shem Tov, ca. 1700-1760 — Legends. 3. Hasidism. 4. Mysticism Judaism. 5. Title.

ISBN: 978-0-9792865-9-9

BST Publishing
Cleveland, Ohio 44124
www.baalshemtov.com

B"H   14 Adar II 5771

"It is a Mitzvah to publicize those people who perform Mitzvos."

Reb Tzvi Meir HaCohane Cohn, who lives here in Cleveland, has invested tremendous efforts, both monetarily and with his time, to publicize the Torah and stories of the Holy Baal Shem Tov. With regards to his present project of publicizing stories that relate to the weekly Torah portion, I express many thanks and gratitude for his undertaking this wonderful endeavor, L'sheim Shamayim (for the sake of Heaven). To emphasize his holy work, I would like to share with you from the words of the Previous Chabad Rebbe, which are printed in the sefer Igros Kodesh Admur Harayatz ZATZAL , Vol. 6. as follows:

S. B. Chaikin

Rabbi Sholom Ber Chaikin

Igros Kodesh Vol. 6
written by the Previous Rebbe[1]

As the well known story goes, the Tzemach Tzedek[2] once sent his truly brilliant Chassid, the famed Rav Yitzchak Aizik HaLevi Epstein from Homil, to the Rebbe of Ruzhin,[3] regarding matters that pertained to the community. This Chassid, who was one of the educated ones of the Chabad Chassidim, was very interested to learn the ways and customs of the Rhyzhiner Chassidim and especially the customs of the Rebbe, Reb Yisrael of Ruzhin, and therefore he put his incredible mind and heart to observe every little detail of what happened.

The way the Holy Rhyzhiner Rebbe would accept people and read the kvitlach,[4] which was the general way by Chassidim of Poland and Vohlin,

---

[1]Rabbi Yosef Yitzchak Schneerson [1880-1950], the sixth Rebbe of Chabad-Lubavitch.

[2]Rabbi Menachem Mendel Schneerson [1789-1886], the third Rebbe of Chabad-Lubavitch.

[3]Rabbi Yisrael Friedmann of Ruzhin [1797-1850] was a great-grandson of the Maggid of Mezritch. At a young age was already a charismatic leader with a large following of Chassidim. Greatly respected by the other Rebbes and Jewish leaders of his generation, he was - and still is - referred to as "The Holy Rhyzhiner."

[4]Written petitions for blessings and prayers placed on pieces of paper.

was as follows. There would be one chosen Chassid selected from the Chassidic elders by the Rebbe, who would be the translator between the Rebbe and his Chassidim. He was called the "close one". This person would stand on the Rebbe's right side to greet people and receive the kvitlach while the gabbai[1] rishon would stand to the left of the Rebbe.

One of the guests at that time in Ruzhin was one of the great Rabbis in Bukavinya, known as a great scholar, and among the closest followers of the Holy Rhyzhiner Rebbe. He brought his sefer, a book of Torah insights to get a haskomah (approbation) from the Rebbe.

Also among the guests was a Chassid who had gathered stories of Tzaddikim and Chassidim over the years and he also brought a sefer containing a compilation of these stories to get a haskomah from the Rebbe.

The time came when the Rebbe was receiving people and these two, the Rav and the Chassid, were standing before the Rebbe with their books. The designated Chassid intermediary, as instructed by the Rebbe, took both books and read for the Rebbe several random pages from the book of the

---

[1] A person who assists in the running of a synagogue and ensures that the needs are met or an administrator to a rabbi (particularly the secretary or personal assistant to a Chassidic Rebbe).

Rav and then a few stories from the book of the Chassid.

The Rebbe sat there in a state of devekus[1] and then started to speak about the greatness of stories of Tzaddikim and the great impression that these stories make in the Heichalos (chambers) of the Tzaddikim in Gan Eden. And afterwards, he expounded on the Torah insights that had been read to him from the book of the Rav. He then instructed the interpreter to write his haskomah for both of these books.

The Chabad Chassid, Rav Yitzchak Aizik, was carefully observing the unfolding of these events, the manner in which the Rebbe was receiving the people and how he would relate to his followers. He was amazed at the depth of analysis that the Rebbe offered on the insights that were read to him from the book of the Rav.

He was, however, confused by the fact that the Rebbe had addressed his comments and given his haskomah for the story book before commenting on and giving his haskomah for the book of the Rav. He found this to be quite surprising.

Two days later was Rosh Chodesh and the Tzemach Tzedek's Chassid, Reb Aizik, was invited

---

[1]Meditative state of being close to G•d.

to the seudah of Reb Yisroel, the Holy Ryzhiner Rebbe. During the seudah, the Rebbe spoke words of Torah and before the benching[1], he said as follows:

"The Litvish Gaon (referring to Reb Aizik) found it surprising that we first spoke about the stories of the Tzaddikim and only afterwards about the sefer containing chiddushei Torah (insights in Torah), and also, that we gave our approval for an haskomah to the book of stories before the book of chiddushei Torah.

"This, in truth, is a great and old question that was asked by Rashi Hakadosh[2], who was a Goan Olam (world class Torah scholar) in the revealed and hidden aspects of Torah. He asked this same question on the first verse in Bereishis. His question was that the Torah only needed to start from the verse of "This month is for you."[3] What is the reason that the Torah starts with Bereishis? He answered, it is to tell of the strength of His (G•d's) deeds. This refers to the neshamah (soul) which is in every action within creation at every time and at every moment."

---

[1] Prayers after eating a meal.
[2] Rabbi Shlomo Itzhaki (1040-1105).
[3] The first mitzvah given to the Jewish people.

"The Zaide, the holy great Maggid,[1] received from the holy Baal Shem Tov a way to see in everything the neshamah (soul) that is in the body of that thing."

"You understand," he turned to the Chassid, Rav Yitzchak Aizik, "we emulate the order that Hashem gave us in his holy Torah. First, Sefer Bereishis is the stories of Tzaddikim. As the Medrash says, "With whom did Hashem consult, with the neshamos of the Tzaddikim." Only afterwards do we have sefer Shemos in which it is stated "HaChodesh hazeh lachem."[2]

"Both of the authors are Chassidim of stature. Both manuscripts are wondrous chiddushim. The chiddushim of Torah authored by the Rav attest to the great learning and thought that the author brought to light in the Holy Torah. And the stories of the Tzaddikim attest to the great novelty that Hashem brought to light in the world. Therefore, we preceded the haskomah for the sefer of stories of Tzaddikim to that of the haskomah for the sefer of Torah insights."

---

[1] Rabbi Dov Ber of Mezeritch (1704-1772).
[2] "This month is to you" *Exodus 12:2.*

G•D

Dedicated to the millions of Chassidim and their Rebbes, who for nearly three centuries, have cherished and passed these holy stories down to us.

יברכך יי וישמרך

יאר יי פניו אליך ויחנך

ישא יי פניו אליך וישם לך שלום

"May the L•rd bless you and guard you. May the L•rd make His countenance shine upon you and be gracious to you. May the L•rd turn His countenance towards you and grant you peace."

BST
Publishing

SHALOM AND BLESSINGS

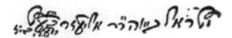

**Yisrael Ben Moreinu Rabbeinu HaRav Rav
Eliezer KoesB (presently in) Mezibush**
Signature of the Baal Shem Tov

BST
Publishing

TABLE OF CONTENTS

INTRODUCTION

The most famous master of Kabbalah[1] and Jewish mysticism is Rabbi Yisrael Ben Eliezer. Rabbi Yisrael lived from 1698 to 1760, and is known as the Baal Shem Tov.[2] More stories are told about the Baal Shem Tov than about any other person in Jewish history. These stories have been passed down, primarily through an oral tradition, for over 250 years. More recently, books — and even more recently the internet — have been added as a means to continue the time-honored tradition of transmitting Baal Shem Tov stories from parent to child and from Chassid[3] to Chassid.

The Baal Shem Tov stories are indeed glimpses of the life and culture of downtrodden, 18th century, Eastern European Jewry. However, to see the stories as only that is to miss their central

---

[1] Jewish Mystical Tradition.
[2] Master of the Good Name.
[3] A Chassid is a pious person — one who goes "beyond the line of the law" in his duties toward G•d and man.

1

role. In Chassidic life, Baal Shem Tov stories have formed the foundation of one of the most fundamental and important of Chassidic spiritual practices: telling stories about the Tzaddikim — the Jewish saints, as it were; literally, the "righteous ones"—the great Spiritual Masters. These Tzaddikim led and guided the various Chassidic dynasties through the dark exile of European Jewry, from the time of the Baal Shem Tov.

All Chassidim, irrespective of their particular allegiance — whether to Chabad, Bretslov, Aleksander, Belz, Satmar, Gerrer, Vishnitz, to name a few — share one common belief: that the basic facts of the Baal Shem Tov stories are just that — facts. There is an old Chassidic saying: "If you believe all of the Baal Shem Tov stories you're a fool; if you don't believe any of them you are a bigger fool."

Today, the stories and teachings of the Baal Shem Tov are as relevant as they were in the past. They inspire and guide us. They nudge us towards intensifying our service to G•d.[1] The stories teach through example how to live our life with a joyful attitude. They enable us to experience the flow of love that emanates from G•d.

---

[1] It is a practice among practicing Jews not to spell out the Name of the Almighty.

INTRODUCTION

I would like to express my gratitude to many people who have made this book possible.

Rabbi Sholom Ber Chaikin for reading the manuscript of this book, checking for errors and catching various mistakes of fact and occasionally tone.

To my ever supportive wife and muse Basha, thank you.

May G•d, blessed be He, shower blessings on all those who have helped in the preparation of this book.

PREFACE

BAAL SHEM TOV literally means, "Master of the Good Name." How appropriate an appellation for Rabbi Yisrael Ben Eliezer, who was to become the founder of the Chassidic movement — the single most important religious movement in Jewish history! We know that he was born on the 18th of Elul in 1698 and left this world on Shavuos, the 6th of Sivan 1760, but little other verifiable biographical information has come down to us. Moreover, the Baal Shem Tov's life is so overlain with legend, it is difficult to determine what is true of the information we *do* have.

According to the stories, Rabbi Yisrael's parents were poor, righteous, and hospitable. When he was orphaned at a very young age, the Jewish community of Horodenka took him under its wing,

5

fed and clothed him, and enrolled him in the local cheder.[1]

He is described as an unusually sensitive child, and quite early demonstrated a profound attachment to G•d and to nature. He often wandered in the forests and fields surrounding the village, and spent many hours there, alone, close to the natural world, talking to G•d.

At the age of twelve, he began working as the local cheder teacher's assistant. His job was to bring the students to and from school and to review their lessons with them. Later, he served as a shamash,[2] a shochet,[3] and worked as a laborer.

Unbeknownst to others, he was also devoted to Torah study and became extremely learned as a Talmid Chacham and Kabbalist.

The man who was to become the Baal Shem Tov so successfully concealed his spiritual and scholarly achievements that the great Talmudist, Rabbi Avraham Gershon of Kitov, vehemently opposed R. Yisrael's marriage to his sister, Chana. Rabbi Avraham Gershon viewed Rabbi Yisrael, who maintained a pretense of humble ignorance, as unworthy of their family. They did, however, marry, and after they had wed, Rabbi Yisrael worked as a

---

[1] A Hebrew day school for young boys.
[2] A caretaker of the synagogue.
[3] A ritual slaughterer.

clay digger, a wagon driver, an inn keeper, and a healer.

In fact, the Baal Shem Tov (also know by the acronym the Besht) was part of a group of hidden holy men and mystics who worked among the "Jewish masses." Certainly, in that place and time, the majority of Jews were ignorant of Torah. By moving among the common Jewish folk without revealing their status as learned men, these hidden "Saints" were able to relate easily to those they would later lead.

From his twenty-sixth to his thirty-sixth birthday, the Baal Shem Tov studied the deepest secrets of the Torah with Achiyah the Shilonite. Achiyah HaShiloni is described as a Heavenly teacher — one who was a Biblical Prophet and the teacher of both King David and Elijah the Prophet.

During Rabbi Yisrael's years of travel as a hidden Saint, he had learned a great deal about folk remedies. Eventually, he combined his practical knowledge of herbs and healing with his mastery of Kabbalah, and his first public appearance was as a Baal Shem — the name given to a few, select, Jewish miracle rabbis that used mystical powers engendered by the Kabbalah, to heal the ill, ward off demons, and predict future events. The Baal Shem Tov was distinguished from the other Baal Shems, and the first to be called Baal Shem Tov because of his remarkable spiritual powers including the ability to see events from afar, predict the future, and look into someone's previous incarnations to help those seeking relief from ailments of the body and soul.

The Baal Shem Tov took to visiting the nearby towns and hamlets of Podolia, Volhynia, and Galicia, and began preaching the tenets of Chassidism. The most fundamental teaching of Chassidism, as taught by the Baal Shem Tov, is the omnipresence of G•d. The whole universe is a manifestation of the Divine. This manifestation is not an "Emanation" but a "Portion" of G•d; nothing is separate from G•d. Divine (G•d's) providence is a mantle over all. Therefore, everything in creation, including man, animals, plants and even inanimate objects are directly supervised by G•d.

It follows, then, that all things possess an inner spark of holiness — even something or someone we perceive as evil. Every person, no matter how far he or she has strayed from the ways of G•d, is capable of return; no sinner is damned. The Baal Shem Tov's teachings emphasized constant communion with G•d, and the enthusiasm and joy that are essential to an experiential relationship with Him. These ideas were not altogether new to Judaism, but the manner in which they were presented was little short of revolutionary. The Baal Shem Tov spoke directly to the masses of unlearned[1] Jews. Their task, he told them, was not to be something they were not — for example, learned Talmudists. Rather, their task was to infuse their daily lives with spiritual meaning.

The Baal Shem Tov taught that since G•d's providence extends to all of creation, everything is created and continues to exist because of His intention. As G•d is everywhere and in all things, all actions must be performed with an awareness of His presence, as well as with the love and joy that are integral to such awareness. One's goal in life should be to construct for the Holy One, Blessed be He, a habitation in this physical world. Through this, we will merit to bring the Moshiach, so that the world will be in accordance with G•d's plan.

The following was said by the Rebbe Maharash (fourth Rebbe of Chabad-Lubavitch 1832-1882): "The world makes three errors by thinking that telling stories of the Baal Shem Tov on Motzoei Shabbos[2] ensures one's livelihood. First

---

[1] Unschooled in Judaism.
[2] After Shabbos ends.

of all, these stories are not to be limited to the Baal Shem Tov, but should include tales of all our Tzaddikim. Secondly, they should not be told only after Shabbos but at any time. And lastly, telling these stories not only ensures livelihood, but serves as a Segulah[1] to ensure we receive an abundance of blessings relating to our children, good health and success in our livelihood."

This teaching of the Rebbe Maharash is believed and acted on by all the various groups of Chassidim and is part of the reason I collected and freely adapted and published the stories in this book. By reading and telling these stories to others, you are promised by a long chain of Chassidic rebbes that you will receive abundant blessings relating to your children, good health and success in your livelihood.

Please tell these stories to others and give this book to others in order to fulfill the requirement of the Moshiach for the Baal Shem Tov's teachings to become publicly known and revealed throughout the world, and his wellsprings (Torah from the source) dispersed throughout the

---

[1] An action that is reputed to lead to a change in one's fortunes.

PREFACE

world so that the Moshiach will quickly reveal
himself.

CHAPTER ONE

DEVARIM

"And like you have seen how G•d, your G•d, has carried you in the desert like a man carries his son . . . ." *Devarim 1:31*

A SPEEDY JOURNEY

AND then there was the time that Reb Michel of Ostropol, a great Torah sage and respected by all, received news that his close friend and colleague Reb Yankel would be making a bris for his newly born son, on the coming Friday. As Reb Michel and Reb Yankel were as close as brothers, Reb Michel decided that he would attend.

Besides being known as a great Torah sage, he was also known to be a fastidious and nervous man. So, as he began to ponder the anticipated trip, he became nervous. "Reb Yankel's village is a half day's travel from Ostropol," he thought. "How will I be able to go the bris and still have enough time to return home for Shabbos? I know. I will send Reb Yankel a message requesting that he make the bris as early as possible so I can return home to Ostropol in time for Shabbos."

A few days later, Reb Michel received a message from Reb Yankel agreeing to make the bris early in the morning. Reb Michel traveled to Reb

Yankel's village Thursday morning allowing plenty of time for any delays. He immediately went to the home of Reb Yankel where they warmly greeted each other and celebrated the good news.

By early the next morning, preparations for the bris had been completed so that Reb Michel could return home in time for Shabbos.

Suddenly, a wagon full of Chassidism pulled up in front of Reb Yankel's house. It was the Baal Shem Tov and his disciples who had come to participate in the joyous event. Reb Yankel was overjoyed with this unexpected surprise of his Rebbe and the accompanying Chassidim.

As it was the custom of the Baal Shem Tov to immerse himself in a mikveh before morning prayers, the bris had to be delayed until he returned. The Baal Shem Tov did not rush his immersion, or his walk to and from the mikveh.

The bris was finally held several hours after the intended starting time. The seudah took longer than expected as the Chassidim sang song after song, exchanged Torah thoughts and rejoiced. Reb Michel was so overjoyed to be celebrating such a wonderful Simcha, and in the company of Chassidim, that he forgot the time. When the festivities were finally over, he looked at his watch and saw to his horror that there was less than an hour until candle lighting time for Shabbos.

Reb Michel began to panic: "What shall I do?" he thought to himself in despair. As he began to pace the floor, the Baal Shem Tov approached him.

"Reb Michel," he began, "why are you so worried about time? Time is a creation like anything else. If the Almighty has created it for us, then it is to be used to serve Him. Do you think that you have somehow lost time because of our joyous celebration for the sake of the great occasion of a bris? If I arranged for you to arrive home in time for Shabbos, will you allow me and my Chassidim to be your guests this Shabbos?"

"But of course!" exclaimed Reb Michel in a daze. The Baal Shem Tov quickly instructed his Chassidim to climb into their wagon, and sat Reb Michel by his side. The wagon driver Alexei snapped the reins and the horses were off on the road to Ostropol. After fifteen minutes of travel, the Baal Shem Tov turned to the bewildered Reb Michel and said, "Look Reb Michel, we're already approaching Ostropol, and you still have forty five minutes to spare to prepare for the holy Shabbos."

The wagon stopped in front of Reb Michel's house. Still unsure of what had just transpired, he quickly stepped down from the wagon and welcomed his honored guests into his home. It was a memorable Shabbos, and from that day, Reb Michel became an ardent Chassid of the Baal Shem Tov.

And so it was.

"Do not fear them, for it is G•d, your G•d, Who is fighting for you." *Devarim 3:22*

THE MAGIC MIRROR

AND it happened that once while traveling, Rabbi Schneur Zalman (known as the Alter Rebbe)[1] was in a city when a house caught on fire. When the Alter Rebbe arrived at the scene of the fire, a group of Russian soldiers were trying unsuccessfully to extinguish it. The Rebbe stood in front of the blazing house, leaned on his cane and gazed for a few moments into the fire. Suddenly, the fire died down and was easily extinguished.

The exhausted soldiers could barely believe their eyes. They ran to report the astonishing event to their General. After hearing their story, he sent a group of soldiers to ask the Rabbi to come and see him. When the Alter Rebbe arrived, the General asked him, "Are you any relation to the Jewish holy man known as the Baal Shem Tov?"

The Rebbe replied, "Sir, while I'm not a blood relative, I consider myself to be his spiritual grandson because I am a disciple of the Maggid of

---

[1] The Alter Rebbe (1745-1812), the first Rebbe of Chabad.

Mezritch, the Baal Shem Tov's successor. Why do you ask?"

"When I heard how the fire was brought under control after you gazed at it for a few moments, it reminded me of a story that happened to my father.

"My father was also a general. Once he was stationed with his troops in the village of Mezibush. At that time, my father was deeply troubled because many weeks had passed since he had received a letter from his wife. He started to have all kinds of bad thoughts. This caused him to be in a very bad mood which he took out on his troops. One of his officers suggested that he should seek the advice of a local Jewish holy man, known as the Baal Shem Tov, who was reputed to be a miracle worker. 'Maybe he'll be able to tell you some news about your wife,' said the officer.

"My father, although still in a foul mood, agreed and sent this very officer to arrange a meeting between him and the Baal Shem Tov. Much to my father's surprise, the gabbai[1] of the Baal Shem Tov told the officer that the Baal Shem Tov refused to see him. So my father sent a higher ranked officer, but the Baal Shem Tov again refused to see him. By this time, my father was infuriated

---

[1] Person who assists in the running of a synagogue.

that this simple rabbi refused to see his officers and of course himself, the commanding officer, a general no less. My father knew about Jewish customs and holidays. At that time, it was right before Passover. So he sent another officer to relay the threat to the Baal Shem Tov that if he did not grant him an interview, he, being the General, would quarter his troops in Jewish homes. This would cause bread and even non-kosher food to be brought into the Jewish homes just before Passover.

"The threat worked and the Baal Shem Tov sent back a message inviting my father to his home. When my father arrived, he entered a waiting room and saw the Baal Shem Tov through an open doorway, sitting in his study. He was absorbed in a book which my father later found out was a kabbalistic book called the Zohar. However, before my father even knocked on the door to the study, his attention was caught by a large mirror on the wall in the waiting room.

"He went over to the mirror to adjust his clothes before meeting the Rabbi. When he looked into the mirror, to his astonishment, he saw the road leading to his own city, instead of his own reflection. As he watched the road, the scene changed and he saw his own house. Suddenly he could see into his house. There his wife was sitting at a table and writing a letter to him. He was able to clearly see the letter. She was writing an apology for having not written sooner. She explained that it was due to her difficult pregnancy and delivery of a baby boy. Everything was fine.

"My father was overwhelmed by the vision in the mirror. When he met with the Baal Shem Tov, he thanked him profusely. A few days later, he received a letter from his wife, identical to what he had seen in the mirror. My father then wrote down the whole story in his personal diary.

"I," concluded the General to Rabbi Schneur Zalman, "am the son whose birth was announced in that letter! Also, I always carry with me the diary in which my father recorded this event."

And so it was.

CHAPTER TWO

VA'ESCHANAN

"[Also] write them on [parchments affixed to] the doorposts of your house and upon your [public] gates." *Va'eschanan 6:9*

THE DEFECTIVE MEZUZAH

AND it happened that once, that the Baal Shem Tov was visiting the home of a member of the Holy Community of Nemirov. While going from one room to another room, the Baal Shem Tov "inadvertently" opened the door to the cellar. He reached out to kiss the Mezuzah affixed to the cellar doorway.[1] But before he actually touched the Mezuzah, he suddenly stopped. Rabbi Yisrael looked over to his host and said, "This Mezuzah should be checked."[2]

The host replied, "Rabbi, just because you opened the wrong door, does that mean you need to justify your mistake by questioning the kashrus of

---

[1]It is an age old Jewish custom to touch a Mezuzah with your finger tips and then kiss them.
[2]Mezuzahs need to be checked every few years because the inked letters can break or peel off, or even touch each other due to shrinkage of the klaf on which it is written. Even a slight imperfection in the letters renders the Mezuzah defective and non-kosher.

my Mezuzah? Maybe you just accidentally opened the door to the cellar?"

The Baal Shem Tov answered, "As far as I'm concerned, there is no such thing as an accident. In reality, everything, without exception, is directed by Divine Guidance and is not a matter of chance."

Later, the man found that the Mezuzah was in fact posul.[1]

And so it was.

---

[1] Defective.

"Enough of your (requests!) Do not speak to Me anymore about this matter." *Va'eschanan 3:26*

THE BOOK

WHEN Yisrael Ben Eliezer was fourteen years old, he left the holy community of Horodenka, where the local people had cared for him after the death of his parents, Rabbi Eliezer and Rebbetzyn Sarah.

In time, he wandered back to Okup, the village where he was born. It was then that he discovered a yearning in his heart that was only satisfied by the study of the Holy Torah.

Young Yisrael (then known as Yisroelic) worked as a shamash[1] and lived in the same synagogue where he worked. But, he was very careful not to show his passion for the Torah to anyone. By day, he slept on the benches, and everyone thought he was just an ignorant Jewish boy. But after the last man closed the holy book he was studying and left the synagogue, Yisroelic stood and studied the Holy Torah all night by candlelight.

In another city, Rabbi Adam Baal Shem, an elderly holy Tzaddik dwelled. Years before, Rabbi

---

[1]Synagogue caretaker.

Adam had mastered the Torah and the Kabbalah, but he was still not satisfied. He prayed and prayed, "Dearest G•d, I beg of you to reveal to me the innermost secrets of Your Torah."

One night, Rabbi Adam dreamt that he was in the Maras Machpelah.[1] There, deep in the underground cave, Rabbi Adam was given The Book, the Word of the Ever-Present G•d, and the ability to understand its contents. Until then, this deepest of all knowledge had been possessed by only six others: Adam, Abraham, Joseph, Moses, Joshua Ben Nun, and King Solomon.

From that moment on, Rabbi Adam spent all of his time studying the secret knowledge in The Book. But as he grew older, he began to wonder to whom he would give The Book, when his time came. So he prayed, "Dearest G•d, I must find someone to whom I can pass on this sacred text. Please send me a son to carry on the work."

Soon after, he was blessed with a son. As the son grew, he taught him the Torah and the Kabbalah. But, Rabbi Adam's son did not have an endless thirst for knowledge; he did not merit receiving The Book.

---

[1] A cave in Hebron where Adam and Eve, Abraham and Sarah, Isaac and Rebecca, and Yaakov and Leah are buried.

Not knowing to whom he should pass it on, Rabbi Adam prepared a dream question. "To whom should I give The Book?" he asked each night, just before retiring.

One night the answer came, "Give The Book to Yisrael son of Eliezer, who lives in Okup." When Rabbi Adam awoke, he called his son and gave him The Book. "This book contains the only Torah that I've not studied with you."

"But father," cried his son, "am I not worthy to learn it?"

"I am sorry my son," Rabbi Adam said gently. "It is not you. It is just not for your soul. Take The Book to Yisrael son of Eliezer, who lives in Okup, because The Book belongs to him. Maybe he will accept you as a student and instruct you in this deepest of all Torah."

Soon thereafter, Rabbi Adam passed onto the next world, and Rabbi Adam's son moved to the town of Okup. The local townspeople were puzzled as to why such a great Torah scholar had come to live in their little town. He explained, "Friends, my holy father, Rabbi Adam the Tzaddik, told me to find a wife and settle here in Okup."

Upon hearing that, they exclaimed, "Oh Rabbi, we are thrilled to be blessed with you! And as far as a wife, with G•d's help, it will be arranged soon."

Many marriageable girls were suggested. Rabbi Adam's son married a rich man's daughter and began a routine of studying Torah in the synagogue where Yisrael served as the shamash.

All this time, he looked for a deeply spiritual person named Rabbi Yisrael Ben Eliezer, but was unable to find him.

Eventually, he noticed the boy called Yisroelic, who took care of the synagogue. One night, while pretending to sleep, Rabbi Adam's son saw Yisroelic study a holy book of Torah by candlelight throughout the entire night.

Early in the morning, when the boy lay down on one of the benches to sleep, Rabbi Adam's son took a page of The Book and carefully placed it on Yisroelic's chest. The boy stirred and picked up the page. As he began to read, he awoke fully. His face turned red and his eyes shone bright. He stood up and became totally engrossed in studying the page.

Within a few minutes Rabbi Adam's son knew that he had found Yisrael Ben Eliezer to whom The Book belonged. So he gave him the rest of The Book and explained, "My father, Rabbi Adam the Tzaddik, instructed me to give The Book to you. I beg of you, please take me as your student and teach me the Torah from The Book." Yisrael agreed and they began to study together.

Soon, Rabbi Adam's son asked his father-in-law to hire Yisrael as his helper, and to build him a study house on the outskirts of the village so that he could study without any disruption. His father-in-law agreed. From then on, the two of them poured over The Book in the little study house, devoting themselves to it. They soared through the hidden worlds, exploring the source of the Torah.

In time, Yisrael noticed that Rabbi Adam's son had become thinner and weaker. He asked him what was the problem, but Rabbi Adam's son did not respond. Yisrael was worried about the health of his friend, and he persisted with his questions. Finally Rabbi Adam's son replied, "Yisrael, the more I learn, the greater the emptiness I feel. I need to know the Ineffable Name.[1] Otherwise, I just cannot go on."

Yisrael nodded with understanding but said, "My dearest friend, we are not pure enough to reach the spiritual level where we can obtain that deepest of all knowledge." After that, Rabbi Adam's son no longer asked to know the Name and he continued to become weaker and weaker.

---

[1] 72 letter name of G•d.

In desperation, Yisrael decided to try and learn the Ineffable Name — before his friend simply left the body. "All right," he finally told Rabbi Adam's son, "we will try. May G•d save us."

So they fasted from one Shabbos to another. On Friday afternoon, just before the second Shabbos, they went to the mikveh to purify themselves. After reciting the Shabbos evening prayers, they concentrated on a certain combination of Hebrew letters and entered into a deep trance.

Yisrael prayed with all his might, "Dearest G•d, please reveal to us your ineffable Name!"

Suddenly, they were both jolted back into everyday consciousness. With great concern, Yisrael said to Rabbi Adam's son, "Oh my G•d! We lost our concentration and the Prince of Fire[1] is descending to take us. We only have one hope. We must stay awake all night and study The Book without letting our eyes close with sleep for even a second!"

Rabbi Adam's son looked at Yisrael with fear in his eyes.

Yisrael put his hand on his shoulder and said, "Don't worry, I will help you."

---

[1] The Angel Gabriel.

And so Yisrael and Rabbi Adam's son stood next to each other and read out loud from The Book. But just before morning, Rabbi Adam's son could not keep his eyes open any longer. He fell into a deep sleep from which he never awoke.

And so it was.

CHAPTER THREE

EIKEV

". . . what does G•d, your G•d demand of you? Only to fear G•d, your G•d, to follow all His ways, to love him, to serve G•d, your G•d, with all your heart and with all your soul . . ." *Eikev 10:12*

A BUNDLE OF GREENS

REB Eliezer Lippa was a simple but devout Jewish man who lived in the town of Taranow in Galicia. He was not well versed in Torah and didn't know the meaning of most of the daily prayers, but he always prayed with the minyan and was scrupulous to say all the proper responses to the chazzan.[1] He never conversed about worldly matters in the synagogue and accorded the Torah scholars and his Rabbi their due honor.

Reb Eliezer Lippa worked as a water carrier, one who filled the water barrels located by the front door of every house in the town from the nearby river. He worked hard and managed to make a decent living, as he had four steady customers who were well-to-do merchants and paid him above the average rate for his services.

One day, our saintly Rebbe, the holy Rabbi Yisrael Baal Shem Tov arrived in Taranow. This was

---

[1] Prayer leader.

before the Rebbe had revealed himself to the world, and he appeared as just another of the thousands of simple, wandering beggars, but with a gift for telling stories. In those years, he used to travel from town to town and tell stories from the Talmud to the masses of unlearned Jews. He would also speak to them about how much G•d was pleased with the heartfelt prayers and simple faith of ordinary Jews.

Reb Eliezer Lippa was guiding his wagon with its full barrel of water through the center of town when he spotted his close friend and fellow water carrier Reb Zalman Dov along with some other men, gathered around this simply dressed itinerant man known as Reb Yisroelic and listening intently with their heads inclined to catch his every word.

His interest sparked, Reb Eliezer Lippa went over to join the circle of listeners. The Baal Shem Tov was telling the story related in the Talmud of a wealthy man who lived in the days when the Holy Temple in Jerusalem still stood.

The Baal Shem Tov explained, "A wealthy man was taking a fattened ox to the Temple for a sacrifice. It was a massive beast, and when it decided, for reasons of its own, to stop still in its tracks, nobody was able to convince it to walk further towards their destination. No amount of pushing and prodding could make that animal budge.

"A poor man who was on his way home was watching the scene. In his hand was a bunch of freshly picked greens that he was bringing to his family to eat. These he now held to the muzzle of the ox, and when the animal began to nibble, he slowly drew them away and thereby led the animal to its destination at the Holy Temple.

"That night, the owner of the ox had a dream. In his dream, he heard a voice which called out, 'The sacrifice of the poor man, who gave up the bundle of greens he was bringing to his impoverished family, was a more desirable sacrifice than your fattened ox.'

"The wealthy man," continued the Baal Shem Tov, "had brought a large fattened ox for a burnt offering. And he was so joyful at being able to bring such an animal that he had also brought a sheep for a peace offering. He made a huge feast for his family and friends and also distributed the proper gifts from his sacrifices to the priests. His joy was so great that he held back nothing. The poor man, on the other hand, had only offered the ox a bunch of greens that he intended to bring home for his impoverished family. What were his few stalks compared to the fattened ox, the sheep and the feast of the wealthy man?

"Nevertheless," concluded the Baal Shem Tov, "G•d desires the heart. Any mitzvah a person does, whether great or small, simple or difficult, is judged by how it is performed. A mitzvah done for G•d's sake, with great joy and purity of heart, is very precious to the Holy One blessed be He. G•d cries out to the angels, 'Look at the mitzvah my child has done!' G•d, from his place in the heavens saw that although the wealthy man had offered much of his belongings, the poor man had offered much more of himself."

Reb Eliezer Lippa's mind knew no rest. How he longed to be able to do a mitzvah like the poor man in the story, with pure intention and a joyful overflowing heart! The weeks passed and still Reb Eliezer Lippa knew no peace as his heart ached with the desire to be able to do such a mitzvah.

One day, as Reb Eliezer Lippa was delivering water to one of his wealthy customers, he had an idea, an idea so perfect that his whole being became flushed with a great sense of pleasure and relief. Reb Eliezer Lippa's four wealthy customers provided him with half of his livelihood since they paid him far more than the going rate for a barrel of water. On the other hand, his friend Reb Zalman

Dov supplied the town's four synagogues, which paid him half of the going rate for their water. "I can exchange four of my customers for four of his," thought Reb Eliezer Lippa, "four wealthy homes for four synagogues." He was anxious to serve G•d by providing the water that the congregants would wash their hands with. Certainly the mitzvah of providing for the needs of the men praying to G•d was of more value than the profits he would give up.

He went home and told his wife about the story he heard from the visiting storyteller, and how doing a mitzvah with joy is like bringing a sacrifice in the Holy Temple even though it no longer stands. His wife readily agreed to the idea, as did Reb Zalman Dov who sorely needed the extra income. The deal was struck and the exchange of customers was made.

No one but Reb Eliezer Lippa and his wife knew what had happened and they were overjoyed at the prospects for their new "business." There were days when Reb Eliezer Lippa's wife went to the river to participate in the mitzvah of drawing the water for the synagogues. As they hauled the water, they would concentrate on the mitzvah of preparing the water for the congregants to wash their hands before prayers, and their joy was boundless, for they understood that G•d desires the heart.

Amongst Chassidim, there is a tradition that it was in the merit of their special mitzvah, that Reb Eliezer Lippa and his wife were blessed with children, for she had formerly been barren. They gave birth to two sons, Reb Elimelech of Lizhensc and Reb Zusha of Anipoli, two of the most illustrious disciples of the Baal Shem Tov's successor, Reb DovBer, the Maggid of Mezritch.

Reb Elimelech and Reb Zusha grew to be luminaries who lit up the Jewish world and inspired tens of thousands to return to G•d and to serve Him with joy.

And so it was.

"You should bind them as a sign on your hand, and they should be "totafos" between your eyes."
Eikev 11:18

THE MAGICAL POWER OF TEFILLIN

AND it once happened that the holy Baal Shem Tov was studying Torah in the beis medrash with his close disciples. Suddenly, he became so sick that he was unable to speak.

The disciples became very alarmed. "Rebbe, Rebbe," they cried, "what's wrong? Can we get you something?"

The Baal Shem Tov motioned to his Tefillin bag. Quickly, the students took out his Tefillin and wrapped one around his arm and put the other on his head. By then, the Baal Shem Tov was so weak that he just lay down on a bench. He closed his eyes and didn't move. The disciples sat by his side unsure of what to do. After a long time passed, the Baal Shem Tov sat up and began speaking to the disciples. "Thank G•d, I'm feeling better."

The disciples asked in a concerned voice, "Rebbe, what happened?"

The Baal Shem Tov explained, "In my youth, I committed a sin. An accusation was made against me before the Heavenly Court and the Court decided that I deserve to die. At first, I wasn't aware of what was happening to me. All I knew was that I started to feel very, very weak. Just then, my holy teacher, Achiyah HaShiloni (a Heavenly teacher, a prophet), came and explained to me the situation. Then he told me, 'Yisrael, quickly put on your Tefillin.'

"After you put my Tefillin on," continued the Baal Shem Tov to the disciples, "the Satan came in the form of a Russian peasant carrying an iron shovel in his hand. He wanted to chop off my head. But because of the power of the Tefillin, the Satan could not get close to me. He started yelling, 'Take off that leather!'[1] But I didn't pay any attention to him and he continued yelling until, thank G•d, the accusation was nullified by the Heavenly Court."

The Baal Shem Tov continued, "During that time, my brother-in-law, Rabbi Gershon came to testify for me. However, the gates to the Heavenly Court were closed and he couldn't get through. But that didn't stop Reb Gershon. He took a heavy wooden shaft and started banging on the gates until they were finally opened. Then, he ran in and started yelling before the Court in an angry voice, 'Will you sentence Rabbi Yisrael to death, G•d

---

[1] Tefillin are made of leather.

forbid, for a trivial thing that happened in his youth?' The Court wasn't able to overcome the defense of Reb Gershon and revoked their original sentence."

The Baal Shem Tov continued, "It says in the Tikunei Zohar,[1] the commandment of Matronita[2] places a man under her wings and protects him from the hand of the Accuser. So it is with the commandment of wearing Tefillin."

And so it was.

---

[1] A book of Kabbalah.
[2] The Shechinah — the female aspect of G•d.

CHAPTER FOUR

RE'EH

". . . . you may eat as much meat as your soul desires . . . . . you may (eat) from your cattle and sheep which G•d has given you, (provided that you first) slaughter (them, as) I have commanded you."
Re'eh 12:20-21

THE UNTRUSTWORTHY SHOCHET

AND then there was the time that the Baal Shem Tov was traveling through the countryside, as he often did. It was already Friday afternoon when he came upon a small village. The local rabbi invited the Baal Shem Tov to stay with him for Shabbos and the Baal Shem Tov was happy to accept the invitation.

The Rabbi was so excited, that he rushed to tell his wife, the Rebbetzyn, "Quick prepare a very special Shabbos meal in honor of our guest, the Holy Baal Shem Tov."

"My husband, we are all ready, thank G•d, because I just bought a piece of beef from the shochet.[1] I'll cook an especially good meal for our guest." But when she went to prepare the meat, it was gone. She looked frantically throughout the house but it was nowhere to be found.

---

[1] A Jewish slaughterer that kills the animals in accordance with the requirements of Jewish law.

In desperation, the rebbetzyn asked her next door neighbor to lend her a piece of the roasted meat she had already prepared for Shabbos. Her neighbor agreed but when she went to get the cooked meat, it was also mysteriously missing. Then she went to a second neighbor to borrow a piece of meat, and found her meat was also missing.

In frustration, she returned home to ask her husband what to do. As she walked in the door of her home, she looked out the window and coincidently saw the local shochet walking by on the street.

The rebbetzyn rushed outside and told the shochet her story of woe.

"Don't worry rebbetzyn," said the shochet, "just a few hours ago, I slaughtered a fat calf. It'll be my pleasure to get you a prime piece of meat."

At that very moment, the Baal Shem Tov happened to be walking by. He stopped and was introduced to the shochet by the rebbetzyn. He told the shochet, "You know, I really love to eat the head of a calf. Could you please bring the calf's head to me whole? I'd like to help clean it."

The shochet readily agreed and immediately left. Soon thereafter, he returned to the Rabbi's house with the head of the calf.

The Baal Shem Tov was waiting for the shochet. After the shochet put the calf's head down on the kitchen table, the Baal Shem Tov asked him about the number of teeth a typical calf has in its mouth but the shochet wasn't sure of the number.

The Baal Shem Tov explained, "Some say it's one number of teeth and others disagree and say it's a different number of teeth. Would you please count the number of teeth this calf has?"

The shochet opened the calf's mouth and when he put his hand in to count the teeth, the calf's mouth closed on his hand. And then, the calf's mouth began to close more and more tightly causing the calf's teeth to cut deeper and deeper into the shochet's hand. The shochet started to cry large tears and scream from the pain.

The Baal Shem Tov looked directly into the shochet's eyes and said, "Why are you crying? Isn't the calf dead?"

The shochet started to panic. "Help me, help me!" he pleaded.

The Baal Shem Tov started yelling, "Confess you wicked man! The calf wasn't kosher, was it?"

"I don't know Rebbe, I really don't know!" cried out the shochet, "I never check the lungs (as required by Jewish law) to see if a calf is kosher. Instead, I just decide by chance whether the meat is kosher or not." With that, the calf's mouth went slack and the shochet withdrew his hand.

"You mean you've caused all of your friends in this community to eat treife?"[1] asked the Baal Shem Tov.

The shochet just mumbled, "I guess so." Then he stood there with a blank expression on his face.

When the local rabbi heard the news, he was outraged. He just kept saying over and over, "You mean we've all been eating treife, G•d forbid."

The Rabbi immediately ordered the shochet to resign from his position. By this time, the news had spread throughout the village. First the villagers discussed the open miracle used by the Baal Shem Tov to trap the shochet and then how the shochet had caused them to eat treife. They were all furious with the shochet. The shochet was so embarrassed that he hid at home with his family and planned to sneak out of town as soon as Shabbos was over.

But before the shochet left the town in disgrace, the Baal Shem Tov instructed him what repentance he would have to do to for such a sin.

And so it was.

---

[1] Non-kosher.

"Three times each year, every male among you must appear before G•d, your G•d in the place that He will choose." *Re'eh 16:16*

It was revealed to the Baal Shem Tov that if the two great lights of the world were to meet, they could bring Moshiach and the final redemption. From that time, the Baal Shem Tov desired greatly to go to Eretz Yisrael to meet the great Ohr Hachayim.[1]

THE EXTINGUISHED WESTERN LIGHT

IN the year 1742, the Baal Shem Tov traveled from home in Mezibush to fulfill his long held desire to visit Eretz Yisrael and meet the great Ohr Hachayim. By Pesach, he reached Istanbul. There he prayed at the gravesite of Rav Naftali, a Tzaddik who had attempted the same trip many years before time but had only traveled as far as Istanbul.

That night, Rav Naftali appeared to the Baal Shem Tov in a dream and said, "Reb Yisrael, it has been decreed in Heaven that you are not destined to dwell in Eretz Yisrael. If you are stubborn and

---

[1] Rabbi Chaim ben Etar (1696-1743). A famous Tzaddik, Posuk, and Kabbalist. Published many books including the Ohr Chaim, an explanation on the Chumash.

attempt to continue your journey, you will die here as I did. Return home."

The Baal Shem Tov accepted the decree and embarked upon a ship headed homewards. His ship was captured by pirates, who let him off at the port of Kilya, from where he continued his journey to Mezibush.

Three months later, during the shalosh seudos meal on the Shabbos of parsha Pinchas, immediately after washing his hands and eating a bite of challah, the Baal Shem Tov said with a sigh, "The Western light has been extinguished."

At the Melave Malkah[1] on that motzoei Shabbos, the Chassidim gathered their courage and asked, "Rebbe, what did you mean when you said that 'The Western light has been extinguished?'"

The Baal Shem Tov replied, "The Ohr Hachayim has passed away. He was known in the Heavenly realms as the Western light."

"How does the Rebbe know that?" one Chassid boldly asked.

The Baal Shem Tov answered, "There is a particular kavanah[2] for the recitation of the blessing for washing hands which I have always wanted to know. However, this kavanah was hidden

[1] Meal celebrating the return of the Shabbos Queen to Heaven.
[2] Intention.

from me since only one person in each generation can know it, and the Ohr Hachayim had preceded me and was designated as that person for this generation. This afternoon, as I washed my hands for shalosh seudos, I suddenly became aware of a new kavanah. I immediately understood that the Ohr Hachayim had passed from this world and now I became the guardian of that kavanah."

One other time, the Baal Shem Tov told his Chassidim of another incident relating to the Ohr Hachayim. On the Shabbos that the great Ohr Hachayim departed from this world, his friend in Tiberias, Reb Chayim Abulafia, mysteriously fainted, and remained unconscious for half an hour. When he finally was revived, he announced to his students, 'Today the Ohr Hachayim left this world. I accompanied him until the gates of Gan Eden.'

"What Reb Chayim of Tiberias did not know," the Baal Shem Tov told his Chassidim, "was that the Ohr Hachayim's saintly neshamah remained in Gan Eden only for the duration of the Shabbos. The next day it descended once more to this world. The souls of Tzaddikim," he explained, "receive greater satisfaction from being in this physical world where the soul can serve the Almighty on the lowest physical plane through performing mitzvos and good deeds which bring far greater benefit to this world, and are far more pleasurable to the soul than being in Gan Eden. When Moshiach arrives and G•dliness will be seen and felt by even the most common person, we will yearn for the days previous when we were able to serve the Almighty on the lowest level of physical existence."

The death of the Ohr Hachayim occurred just two days before the bar mitzvah of the future Tzaddik, Reb Leib Sorahs'. It was years later however, before the Chassidim understood that it was the Ohr Hachayim's soul that he received at the time of his bar mitzvah from his saintly teacher, Rebbe Reb DovBer.[1]

And so it was.

---

[1] The Mezritcher Maggid.

CHAPTER FIVE

SHOFTIM

"(Appoint expert judges so that) they should judge the people correctly." *Shoftim 16:18*

FALSE TESTIMONY

ONCE, there were three men, Reb Ezriel, Reb Anshel, and Reb Eliezer, who were partners in a business. Reb Ezriel bought feathers and hides from Russia and Reb Anshel bought similar merchandise from Galicia. The third partner, Reb Eliezer, who was the son of Reb Sholom, the Belzer Rebbe, arranged financing for their ventures and kept the books, auditing all the expenses and income of their various transactions.

For a long time, all went well. Then, for some unknown reason, Reb Ezriel and Reb Anshel asked Reb Eliezer if they could see the books.

"We would like to know where we stand," they said. But when Reb Eliezer refused to show them the ledgers, the two decided to go with their complaint to his father, the Belzer Rebbe, and to see if he could adjudicate the matter.

"I cannot be a judge in this matter," the Rebbe told the men. "I am the father of the accused and I am therefore invalid to judge."

"Nevertheless," the two partners assured him, "we trust your decision even though you have an interest in the matter."

"Very well," said the Rebbe. "But it is late, just before Mincha and there is no time to hear all the details. For now, let me quickly tell you a story that relates to this situation.

The Rebbe began, "There were once two brothers, one rich and one poor. The rich brother had a daughter who was of marriageable age and the poor brother had a son who was a fine Talmud scholar of the same age. It seemed natural, therefore, that after the rich brother had rejected the many offers of marriage for his daughter, the shadchun[1] urged him to take his nephew, the poor brother's son, as a son-in-law. The rich brother agreed and the two were married.

The young man named Yisrael, soon found life under his father-in-law's roof very uncomfortable. Neither his wife nor father-in-law appreciated his occupation with Torah study and would have preferred that he involve himself in business. The situation became tense, so Reb Yisrael decided to leave and become a melamed[2] for the sake of peace for all involved.

---

[1] Marriage broker.
[2] Hebrew teacher for young boys.

Reb Yisrael traveled far, to an isolated village and there became the melamed for the children of a Chassid of the Baal Shem Tov. In time, the Chassid took a trip to visit his Rebbe.

Just as he was about to depart with a group of other Chassidim, Yisrael asked: "Can you kindly mention me to your Rebbe? I have a difficult personal matter that is a great burden. Perhaps the Baal Shem Tov will have some advice for me."

Yisrael's employer did indeed mention his name to the Holy Baal Shem, and returned home with an urgent message. "As soon as we mentioned your name to the Rebbe, he became quite upset. He told us to advise you to immediately return to your home. The Rebbe's words were, 'Reb Yisrael's return involves a serious matter regarding his wife.' We didn't even know you were married?"

"It is a painful story so I did not share it with you," he answered.

Yisrael was skeptical. He questioned the Chassidim, "How would the Rebbe know of me? How does he even know I'm married?"

"Never mind," they insisted, "if the Baal Shem Tov was so adamant about your returning home, you must do as he says. He told us that he looked at the root of your soul and found a danger present. You must not delay. You should leave immediately."

"How can I go home?" Reb Yisrael answered. "My belongings are here and besides, I don't have any money for the journey."

The Chassidim wouldn't take 'No' for an answer. They all quickly contributed funds to hire a wagon and driver to take Yisrael home and even helped Reb Yisrael gather his few belongings and load the wagon.

"What am I doing?" he thought to himself as the wagon bumped along the dirt road. "I wonder if the Chassidim were just trying to get rid of me. I wonder if they even mentioned my named to the Baal Shem Tov. How could he know about me?" Such thoughts filled his mind as he traveled. He had thoughts of stopping the wagon and turning around, but the urgent words of the Baal Shem Tov disturbed him greatly.

Finally he arrived at his hometown. As the wagon came to a stop in front of his house, he hesitated. He finally summoned the courage to knock on the door. A strange man answered the door. "What did you want?" the man asked.

"Is Reb Yisrael's wife at home?"

"She is no longer Reb Yisrael's wife, and she doesn't live here. In fact, she is planning to get married in two days."

Reb Yisrael was shocked. He had never divorced his wife. How could she get married again? He now understood the urgency of the Baal Shem Tov's words. The first thing he must do was to prevent his wife from marrying another man. But how?

Reb Yisrael went to the beis medrash and sat down to think. As he sat, he overheard several of the local beggars talking about the impending wedding. "I can't wait for the feast. It will no doubt be lavish because the bride's father is certainly rich." Yisrael then knew what he had to do. He went immediately to the town rabbi's home. He related his story, insisting that he had never sent his wife a divorce.

The town rabbi remembered and believed Yisrael. "Please stay here while I go to your father-in-law and discuss this matter."

Reb Yisrael's father-in-law had been deceived by an unscrupulous, traveling darshan.[1] The darshan had come to town and realized the rich man's great despair because his daughter had been deserted by her husband. So he approached the girl's father and said, "In my travels, I've met your son-in-law and we became friends. I'm quite sure that I can get him to divorce your daughter. Just

---

[1] One who expounds on the Midrashic teachings of the Torah.

give me power of attorney to act on your behalf and I will take care of everything."

"That would be wonderful! And you can be sure that I will pay you well for your kindness," the rich man told the darshan.

The darshan quickly traveled to another small town some distance away where he was not known. There he found three men of questionable character and honesty who were willing go along with his ruse for a profit. The darshan then went to a Beis Din, claiming that he had recognized a man at the local inn who was sought for abandoning his wife. "His name is Yisrael and he refuses to give his wife a divorce. Her father has asked me to force him to give a divorce at any cost."

The Beis Din was convinced by the darshan's story. They had the man in the inn (one of the three conspirators) apprehended and brought before them. After some "coaxing", the man admitted that he was the husband that had deserted his wife. Then, the two false witnesses (the other two conspirators) were brought to testify that they also knew the man to be the alleged Reb Yisrael, the runaway husband of the rich man's daughter. The Beis Din "managed" to extract a Get, a bill of divorce, which they gave to the darshan, having the power of attorney of the rich man.

The darshan returned to the rich man with the prized bill of divorce.

"How can I repay you for all your efforts?" the rich man asked.

"I do not want any money," said the darshan. "I was just doing a kindness. However, I would appreciate the opportunity to introduce an eligible young man to your daughter. That is all I ask."

The eligible young man just happened to be the darshan's son, and he made a favorable impression on the family. The wedding date was set and plans were made.

Once the real Yisrael spoke to the town rabbi, the rabbi, accompanied by the local police, marched to the rich man's home. The Rabbi explained Yisrael's story and accused the darshan and his son of fraud. The police promptly took the two scoundrels to jail. The rich man realized that he had been deceived but was very happy that the plot had been foiled in time.

Reb Yisrael found that his wife had meanwhile deeply regretted her unloving behavior towards him, and she begged Yisrael to remain as her husband.

"And," concluded the Belzer Rebbe, "they did live happily thereafter. Do you know why I told you this story?" he asked the two men before him. "You,

Reb Anshel, and you, Reb Ezriel, were the two false witnesses and my son Eliezer was Reb Yisrael in a former life. You two owe him a great deal for the shame and discomfort he suffered. I suggest that you increase his share of the earnings and I am sure he will show you the books."

And so it was.

"You should always set a king over you, one whom G•d, your G•d chooses." *Shoftim 17:15*

A JEWISH KING

ONCE, the Baal Ketzos Hachosen (Rabbi Aryeh Leib) asked the Rabbi Tzvi Hirsch, the Rebbe of Ziditchov, "Why are these times so different from the time of the earlier generations, even just a few hundred years ago?"

"I've noticed," continued the Baal Ketzos Hachosen, "that since the Baal Shem Tov has arrived, he has attracted a large number of followers to beliefs that were primarily the teachings of Ari HaKodesh. So Rebbe, how did the Baal Shem Tov attract such a multitude of followers to his teachings when the same teachings weren't so accepted before?"

Reb Tzvi Hirsch answered, "Let me explain with a parable."

There was a country where the king died without designating someone to assume the position of king. The people searched everywhere in the kingdom for a replacement but couldn't find anyone of suitable stature. Finally, they heard of a man from a distant land that had the characteristics of a great king. He was described by all who saw him as handsome, strong, brilliant, wise, and of exceptional character. There were no other men that even came close to this person, especially in brilliance, wisdom and character. Although, the people of this country were seriously considering appointing this man as king, they still hadn't met him and were reluctant to make such an important decision based on rumors.

Then, a highly respected man returned from traveling to that faraway land and reported that he had seen the candidate with his own eyes. He described how special the candidate was, especially his wisdom and character. After hearing the account of the traveler, some people were ready to accept the man as their king. However, most of the people were still reluctant to make such a decision without actually seeing the man themselves.

A wise man living in the country without the king finally took the initiative to bring the candidate to his country for everyone to see. He took the long, arduous journey to the far away land and convinced the candidate to personally come to his country where the people were desperate to find a king. When the man arrived and the people of the country had the opportunity to meet him and see with their own eyes that he was in fact as handsome, strong, brilliant, wise and of exceptional character as they had heard, they immediately crowned him to be their king.

Then Reb Tzvi Hirsch continued, Rabbi Shimon Bar Yochai and his students were like the ones that spread the rumor of the greatness of the man in the parable. They were the first to reveal the secrets of G•d's glory in the holy Zohar to the general population but the Zohar was still a very esoteric book and most people just couldn't understand the meaning of its teachings.

Then the Arizal, as with the highly respected man who returned from traveling to that faraway land in the parable, began to expound on these esoteric teachings that were first publicly taught in the Zohar. But his explanation of these lofty spiritual matters still couldn't be appreciated by most people since they couldn't see or understand them.

And then came the Baal Shem Tov, like the wise man in the parable who took the initiative to bring the candidate to his country. The Baal Shem Tov revealed G•d by showing that G•dliness exits in everything, even this physical world, without exception. But then, the Baal Shem Tov went even further by teaching us how we can embrace G•d's

Holiness with our thoughts and even our everyday speech and action.

Thus the Baal Shem Tov, just like the wise man in the parable, was able to bring the King of Kings before the eyes of all people.

And so it was.

CHAPTER SIX

KI SEITZEI

"Be careful to carry out what is uttered by your lips — whatever you have pledged to G•d, your G•d . . . . . " *Ki Seitzei 23:24*

REB MICHEL'S KAMEYA

REB Michel was getting old. Being a follower of the Baal Shem Tov, he decided to have yechidus[1] with his Rebbe before he passed on to the next world.

During the meeting, he told the Baal Shem Tov, "Rebbe, more than anything, I want to experience spiritual fulfillment in the next world."

The Baal Shem Tov nodded and gestured for him to sit down. Then the Baal Shem Tov wrote out a kameya. When he handed it to Reb Michel, he said, "Always keep this kameya with you and be sure it is with you when you are buried."

Soon thereafter, Reb Michel passed into the next world. As Reb Michel traveled into higher, more sublime spiritual levels, he merely showed the kameya written by the Baal Shem Tov to whoever was there and he was able to proceed without any questions.

---

[1] Private meeting with a Rebbe.

Then, he reached a very lofty spiritual level where he was greeted by an old man with a long flowing white beard and dressed in an all white robe. As before, Reb Michel showed him his kameya.

"I'm sorry," said the old man, "you can't enter this Heavenly chamber."

Reb Michel was confused. After all, up until then, his holy kameya written by the Baal Shem Tov himself allowed him to travel to higher and higher spiritual worlds. So he asked the old man, "Why can't I go into this chamber? Up until now I've been granted access to every Heavenly chamber that I've wanted to visit."

"I don't know. All I know is that I have been ordered not to let you in," said the old man. "But if you wish, I will go in myself and find out why you are not being allowed in." Reb Michel told him, he'd very much like to know why he wasn't allowed in there.

The old man soon returned and explained, "I was told that you made a promise to one of your close friends before you passed from the physical world that you would regularly appear to him in his dreams and describe all your experiences in the spiritual worlds. So far, while you have been appearing to him in his dreams, you have not told him a number of things that you've seen. The only way for you to enter this chamber and continue to even higher levels is to ask your friend to release you from the promise."

More than anything, Reb Michel wanted to continue studying the deeper concepts of Torah in the more sublime spiritual chambers of heaven and to study with the holy Torah masters of past times. So he appeared to his friend in a dream and asked to be released from the promise. Of course the friend greatly enjoyed hearing about the spiritual worlds and was reluctant to agree.

Finally the friend said, "I agree to release you from the promise but only on one condition. As we've discussed many times, I'm hardly a follower of the Baal Shem Tov and I've never really believed that the kameya he gave you helped you get into the Heavenly chambers that you couldn't have already entered. And even after all you've told me about your experiences in the world beyond, I am still not convinced that your special kameya is having any effect. So my condition is that you give me one sure sign of the Baal Shem Tov's greatness. If you do, I will release you from your promise to regularly appear to me in my dreams."

Feeling somewhat dejected, Reb Michel returned to the old man and asked his advice.

"You know that the Baal Shem Tov almost always expounds on the Torah to his followers during the third meal on Shabbos afternoons. The Torah teachings that he discusses are Heavenly Torah thoughts that no human has previously heard. My advice is to reveal to your friend in a dream what the Baal Shem Tov will discuss this coming Shabbos afternoon. Then tell him to go to the Rebbe's third Shabbos meal where he will hear the identical teaching repeated."

So Reb Michel appeared to his friend in a dream and told him the exact Torah teaching that the Baal Shem Tov would deliver on the upcoming Shabbos afternoon.

The next Shabbos afternoon, Reb Michel's earthbound friend forced himself into the Baal Shem Tov's crowded study hall to hear the Torah thoughts he was going to teach.

The Baal Shem Tov looked him directly in the eye and said, "Why are you pushing everyone to get closer? You really don't have to strain yourself to hear my teachings since you've already heard them before?"

Reb Michel's friend stood was awe struck. This was the sign that he had requested. The Baal Shem Tov not only knew what Torah was being taught in Heaven but also what he was thinking! He thought," Reb Michel, I release you from your promise."

From that moment on, Reb Michel's friend became a devoted Chassid of the Baal Shem Tov.

Sometime later, the Baal Shem Tov told his new follower that Reb Michel was a grandson of the old man who had so kindly and accurately advised him.

And so it was.

"He must write her a bill of divorce for her . . . . . ."
Ki Seitzei 24:1

The words of the righteous can change the world.
Divrei Chassidim

THE STRENGTH OF THE TZADDIK'S WORDS

IN 1740, the Baal Shem Tov came to visit the city of Slutsk. Many of the local inhabitants came to greet him. Among them was the aged scholar, Reb Unna Nosson Natta, who as a youth was known as the Ilui[1] of Karina.

His son, Reb Shlomo who had initially been educated at home by his father, left home at the age of fourteen to seek the scholarly environment of Yeshivas — first in Vilna, then in Jordna, and then in Cracow. There he had met a prominent scholar, Reb Menachem Aryeh, who was a hidden Tzaddik. Reb Menachem accepted him as his disciple in the study of Chassidus on condition that their connection is kept secret.

At the age of twenty-two, Reb Shlomo returned to his childhood home in Slutsk. His father was overjoyed with his progress in learning and arranged a marriage with the daughter of Reb

---

[1] Genius.

Eliyahu Moshe, the leaseholder of an inn located in a nearby village. Tragically, about a half a year after their marriage, the young wife lost her sanity. Since she was not in a mental state to legally accept a bill of divorce, Reb Shlomo was unable to remarry.

During the Baal Shem Tov's visit to Slutsk, Reb Shlomo's father, Reb Unna Nosson Natta, described their sad situation and asked for his advice and blessing. Soon thereafter, the unfortunate young woman's father, Reb Eliyahu Moshe approached the Baal Shem Tov and asked for his advice and a blessing for her recovery.

Later the same day, the Baal Shem Tov invited both fathers to meet with him together. He politely asked if either of them bore a grudge against the other. The bridegroom's father, Reb Unna Nosson Natta, had nothing but praise for his mechutan, the bride's father. He proudly described that despite the pressure of business, the innkeeper fixed times for the study of Torah, maintained a hospitable house that was open to all corners, supported Talmudic scholars generously, and maintained his son-in-law in the most respectable manner.

Since Reb Shlomo had been mentioned, Reb Eliyahu Moshe now spoke most highly of his noble character. He was clearly proud of his son-in-law, who throughout his stay in the village always found time on weekdays to conduct study circles for the simple farming folk who lived round about, teaching them Chumash with Rashi's commentary, and the moral lessons of Ayn Yaakov; and on Shabbos he would read for them from the Midrash and the Ethics of the Fathers. While teaching, he imbued them with a brotherly love for each other, explaining to them that no man's profit ever came at the expense of that which Divine Providence had destined for another. In a word, he was well loved by the villagers from all around. They were saddened by his present plight, and prayed that his young wife would be restored to complete health, and that he would return to teach them as in happier times.

The Baal Shem Tov listened carefully to them both, and then said, "With G•d's help, I will be able to help the young woman return to complete health and restore her mind to its original clarity — but only on one condition: That when this happens the young couple not live together, and when several days have passed, and she is in a fit state according to the Torah Law to accept a Get,[1] she accepts a divorce from her husband with a willing heart."

[1] Bill of divorce.

The two fathers were stunned! The aged father of Reb Shlomo proposed various legal objections to such a divorce, and Reb Eliyahu Moshe argued that his daughter would be grieved by such a procedure, since she respected her husband so highly. He was certain that his son-in-law would likewise be distressed. He himself was prepared to contribute an enormous sum to charity — in the merit of which he begged the Baal Shem Tov to pray for her recovery, but to allow the young couple to rejoin each other in the love and harmony to which they were accustomed. The Baal Shem Tov answered unequivocally — that if they did not agree to the condition that he had stipulated, he would not be able to help them.

A few days later, they called on the Baal Shem Tov together with the young Reb Shlomo, and told him that they accepted his condition — though of course they could not guarantee that his young wife would agree. Upon hearing their reply, the Baal Shem Tov instructed Reb Eliyahu Moshe to immediately go home and tell his sick, ailing daughter that the Baal Shem Tov had come to Slutsk and had requested for her to come to speak with him about an important matter.

Hearing that, the two fathers looked at each other in amazement.

"But Rebbe, for the last six years," Reb Eliyahu Moshe said with a questioning voice, "she has not uttered a single syllable! She just sits between the stove and the wall, and can barely be fed. In a word, my poor daughter is utterly out of her mind. How can I possibly explain to her your request?"

But the Baal Shem Tov did not reply.

Making his way homeward with a heavy heart, Reb Eliyahu Moshe remarked to his mechutan that if the Baal Shem Tov had seen the state in which his daughter was to be found, he would not have spoken as he had. And from the very depths of his heart, Reb Unna Nosson Natta sighed in sympathy for everyone suffering from this matter.

Not so his son, Reb Shlomo. Before his marriage, when he had been a disciple of Reb Menachem Aryeh, he had been introduced to teachings of the Baal Shem Tov. Now that he had met him in person, and had heard his teachings, he became attached to him with all his heart. He therefore told his father-in-law that he thought they should explicitly follow the instructions of the Baal Shem Tov. Reb Unna Nosson Natta added that since they had already accepted the far more difficult condition of their daughter being crazy, they should certainly proceed to carry out the instruction that they attempt to speak to the young woman.

Opening the door to his house, Reb Eliyahu Moshe found his daughter sitting in her accustomed corner behind the stove. He told his wife all that the Baal Shem Tov had said, adding that he was widely reputed to be a great Tzaddik.

To their amazement, their daughter suddenly rose from her place as soon as she heard her father's words. She approached her mother and father quietly, and in a voice they had not heard for six years, asked who was this person who worked wonders. They told her that the man about whom they were speaking was named the Baal Shem Tov, a renowned Tzaddik. She answered that before hearing any more, she first wanted to immerse herself in a mikveh for purification.

After going to the mikveh, the young woman began eating, speaking and sleeping as if completely normal, though she felt very weak. On the third day, she had a high fever and in her delirium spoke about the Baal Shem Tov. When her father heard her crying and asking to be taken to the wonder-worker, he was suddenly reminded of what this turn of events made him forget — that the Baal Shem Tov had asked to see her. He told her of the Baal Shem Tov's request and she was visibly happy to receive the message. On the very next day, accompanied by her parents, she made the journey to Slutsk.

Meanwhile, Reb Shlomo had heard by now of his wife's recovery, for his father-in-law had sent a special messenger with the news. He now began to speak with his father about the principles of Chassidus taught by the Baal Shem Tov. He explained the emphasis which the Baal Shem Tov gave to the mystical teachings of the Kabbalah; the workings of Divine Providence not only for man, but even regarding all created things; the intrinsic holiness and worth of even the simplest fellow Jew; the importance and obligation of Ahavas Yisrael;[1] serving G•d with a joyful heart; and so on.

The aged scholar pondered these matters all day and throughout the following night. On the next day, he set out to Slutz to meet with the Baal Shem Tov. During the meeting, they discussed what his son had told him of his teachings and that he desired to become his disciple. At the same meeting, he told the Baal Shem Tov of the good news about the ailing wife of his son. The Baal Shem Tov replied that on that same day the young woman was again unwell, but that when her father

---

[1] Love of a fellow Jew.

would carry out his mission she would recover and come to see him.

When the young woman and her parents arrived at Slutsk, she and her husband entered the room of the Baal Shem Tov, who told them that they would have to divorce. With bitter tears, the unfortunate young woman told the Baal Shem Tov how highly she respected her husband for his refined character. If, however, he decreed that they should divorce, he must surely know that she was unworthy of such a righteous husband, and felt it her duty to comply. Reb Shlomo, likewise moved, told the Baal Shem Tov that his wife exemplified all the noble attributes by which the Sages define a good wife. If, however, the Baal Shem Tov ordered that they divorce, he too would be agreeable.

The Baal Shem Tov arranged to see them in four days; he would then arrange the legalities required for the divorce.

For the next three days the young couple and their parents fasted and prayed. When on the fourth day, with heavy hearts, they made their way to the Tzaddik, they found a Rav, a scribe and two witnesses already waiting. The Baal Shem Tov asked them if they agreed wholeheartedly to the divorce. They answered that they believed that whatever the Baal Shem Tov told them would be for

KI SEITZEI

the best, and since they loved each other, each of them was willing to proceed with the divorce — for the sake of the other.

The Baal Shem Tov retired to another room and stayed there for some time.

When he returned he related the following story: "Six years ago a threat of terrible suffering hung over your lives because of accusations of the Heavenly prosecuting angel. The Heavenly Court's verdict was that you should both undergo the troubles that you have experienced these last six years. But now you have shown great faith in my words, even to the extent that you were both willing to proceed with a divorce. This very faith has reversed the decree of the Heavenly Court and the charge against you has been annulled. Live on happily together as man and wife. May you be blessed with a home filled with sons, daughters and many grandchildren, and may you both live to a ripe old age."

And so it was.

CHAPTER SEVEN

KI SAVO

".... when you enter the land .... " *Ki Savo 26:1*

When the soul descends from its Heavenly source into 'the land' – it comes into this physical world to fulfill its purpose. *Chassidic teaching*

CHAI ELUL

The Baal Shem Tov was born on Chai Elul in 5458 (1698). On his birthday in 5484 (1724), 26 years later, his Heavenly teacher and spiritual master Achiyah HaShiloni appeared to him. After studying with Achiyah HaShiloni for ten years, the Baal Shem Tov became revealed to the world on his birthday in 5494 (1734).

The Alter Rebbe (Rabbi Schneur Zalman) 5505 (1745), the first Rebbe of Chabad — Lubavitch was born on Chai Elul. *HAYOM YOM compiled by Rabbi Menachem Mendel Schneerson o.b.m.*

THE BAAL SHEM TOV AND THE BIRTH OF SCHNEUR ZALMAN

IN a small shtetl in Poland, during the times of bloody pogroms and fierce anti-Semitism, there lived what appeared to be a simple Jew by the name of Reb Boruch, and his wife Rivkah. Actually, Reb Boruch was a Tzaddik nistar and one of the members of a group of Tzaddik nistars that included the Baal Shem Tov.

Reb Boruch and his wife Rivkah had been married for some years but had not been blessed with a child. At the prompting of his wife, Reb Boruch traveled to his Rebbe, the Baal Shem Tov, for a blessing. He traveled many miles in the freezing, snowy winter to reach Mezibush, the home town of the Baal Shem Tov. There the holy Tzaddik indeed blessed Reb Boruch and his wife Rivkah that they merit to be blessed with a child, and added the words that the child "should reveal Heavenly light hidden in this world."

Soon thereafter, Rivka became pregnant and on Chai Elul — the eighteenth day of the month of Elul, twelve days before Rosh Hashanah —the same birthday as that of the holy Baal Shem Tov, Rivka gave birth to a baby boy whom they named Schneur Zalman.

On that day, the Baal Shem Tov's Chassidim took note of the particularly jubilant mood of their Rebbe. He led the daily prayers with deep kavanah, and afterwards a festive meal was held at which the Tzaddik sang lively niggunim and even danced with unusual joy.

During the festive meal, the Baal Shem Tov said, "Today a neshamah chadasha (a new soul that had not previously occupied a physical body) has come into the world. This soul will illuminate the world by spreading Torah and Chassidus to sustain the spiritual well being of the Jewish people and will bring closer the coming of the Moshiach."

After Yom Kippur, as is the tradition of Chassidim, Reb Boruch visited his Rebbe and requested a blessing for his newly born son. The Baal Shem Tov asked Reb Boruch to keep the news of the birth of his new son secret, and also gave specific instructions for the care and education of his child. In the following weeks, the Chassidim noted that the Baal Shem Tov mentioned the name Schneur Zalman three times during his Torah discourses.

The following year, Reb Boruch again returned to visit his Rebbe for the Yom Tov holidays. The Baal Shem Tov was very interested in the growth of young Schneur Zalman, and asked Reb Boruch specific questions about the child. Again the Baal Shem Tov warned Reb Boruch not to talk to others about their son, particularly regarding his apparent intelligence — as is the nature of parents.

The following year, Reb Boruch again came to the Rebbe for Yom Tov and the Baal Shem Tov again asked many questions about the welfare of the child. Before departing for home, Reb Boruch told the Rebbe that G•d willing, on his next visit, when the child would turn three years old, he would bring his Schneur Zalman with him.

On the following Chai Elul, young Schneur Zalman was brought by his mother Rivkah and his aunt Devorah Leah to the Baal Shem Tov to celebrate little Schneur Zalman's Upscherinish.[1] The Baal Shem Tov appeared very pleased at the joyous event. He cut some of the boy's locks, and then placing his holy hands on the boy's head, blessed little Schneur Zalman with the words of the Birchas Kohanim.[2]

During their visit, young Schneur Zalman asked his mother who was the "old" man that had been the first to cut his hair. As the Baal Shem Tov requested, his mother told him he was his zaida.[3] Following the joyous event, the Baal Shem Tov asked the child's mother and aunt to return home and not to reveal the events of the day.

Later on that day of Chai Elul, there was a special gathering of the Chassidim in celebration of the Baal Shem Tov's birthday. The Baal Shem Tov mentioned that the Torah tells us that at three

---

[1] The first cutting of a boy's hair at three years old.

[2] Numbers 6:24-6:26.

[3] Jewish for grandfather. This term has been used until this day by Chassidim when speaking of the Baal Shem Tov.

years of age Avraham Avinu[1] recognized that there was one G•d. The Baal Shem Tov continued: "There is a great Neshamah in Poland that today reached the age of three years old and has recognized the Creator. He too will undergo mesirus nefesh to reveal a new teaching of the holy Torah that will touch the souls of all Jews."

At that time, there lived a great Torah scholar named Rabbi Yissochar Dov of Kalbink. The Baal Shem Tov arranged for him to be young Schneur Zalman's teacher, but asked Reb Yissochar Dov not to tell Schneur Zalman that the Baal Shem Tov had sent him.

Under the watchful eye of the Baal Shem Tov, the young Schneur Zalman flourished in his studies. He later became one of the 'Chevraya Kadisha' – The Holy Brotherhood of disciples of the Maggid – who would spread the teachings of Chassidus through Eastern Europe, and later become known as 'The Alter Rebbe" — the first Rebbe of the Chabad — Lubavitch Chassidim.

And so it was.

---

[1] Patriarch Abraham.

"As long as you listen to the voice of G•d your G•d, the following blessings will come to bear on you. . . G•d will cause your enemies who rise up against you to be beaten. . . ." *Ki Savo 28:1, 28:7*

THE TRANSFERENCE

THERE was a very rich man who lived with his family in the state of Walachia. Without warning, both of his wife's hands became paralyzed so that she could not move her fingers at all. The man, who was very rich, spared no expense in taking her to all of the most famous physicians that lived in and nearby their city. But alas, none had any idea as to the cause of her illness or a suggestion for a cure.

The husband was not willing to give up. He traveled with her in their carriage from one distant city to another in the hope of finding a physician who that could heal her.

As they traveled, they stayed at inns along the way. At each inn, the condition of his wife and their search for a physician who could heal her was a frequent topic of discussion. Many fellow travelers suggested that they visit Rabbi Yisrael Baal Shem Tov, a famous miracle worker who lived deep in the

Carpathian Mountains. The couple had never heard of the Baal Shem Tov and were hesitant to visit him, especially since he lived so far away in the holy community of Mezibush. But after months of traveling, they agreed that since they were unable to find a doctor who had even an inkling as to the cause of her illness, they might as well visit the Holy Rabbi.

As soon as they arrived in Mezibush, the husband and wife immediately went to meet with the Baal Shem Tov in his study. After they talked for a while, the Baal Shem Tov told them to remain in the community.

The couple found a comfortable inn and stayed for several weeks. During this period of time, they met with the Baal Shem Tov on several occasions. Each time, the Baal Shem Tov told them to stay longer. The husband and wife were both skeptical as to whether the Baal Shem Tov could heal the wife, but they really didn't have a better option. And besides, wherever they went in Mezibush, there was always someone that told them a miracle story about the Baal Shem Tov. Also, everyone assured them that the Baal Shem Tov would heal her.

Finally, after a number of weeks had already passed, the Baal Shem Tov asked Alexi, his wagon driver, to harness the horses to his wagon and prepare for a long trip. Then, he told the man to put his wife in their carriage and to follow him. The man didn't have any idea where they were going but he immediately harnessed his horses to his carriage, put his wife in and followed closely behind the Baal Shem Tov's wagon.

After several days of travel, the wagon and the carriage stopped in front of an inn whose innkeeper was one of the Baal Shem Tov's followers. The noise of the wagon and carriage brought the innkeeper and his wife out to welcome the unknown guests. When the Baal Shem Tov got down from the wagon, the innkeeper was beside himself when he realized it was his Rebbe. The Baal Shem Tov asked the innkeeper whether they could have several rooms for the night.

"Of course Rebbe," the innkeeper answered without hesitation.

"There is one thing," the Baal Shem Tov continued, "during our stay, you will have to lock all the windows and the doors to the inn. And most importantly, you can't open them for anyone, irrespective of who it is, even if it is a very important person. If anyone forces their way in, you should tell him that the Baal Shem Tov ordered the doors and windows locked and then point them to me."

The innkeeper was perplexed by this request, but he promised to carry out every detail of the Baal Shem Tov's instructions. So Alexei unharnessed the horses from the wagon and the carriage, put them in the barn and fed them. Meanwhile, the Baal Shem Tov and the couple carried their bags into the inn. Even before they got settled in their rooms, the innkeeper locked all of the windows and the doors to the inn.

After dinner, they all went to sleep except the Baal Shem Tov who sat at the dining table in the main room and studied from a Holy book. Also, the wife with the paralyzed hands couldn't sleep so she sat next to the warm oven in the corner of the main room.

Coincidently, on that very same day, the regional Governor who owned the inn, was visited by his brother whom he had not seen for many years. They rejoiced at seeing each other by eating and drinking to excess. Being somewhat tipsy from the drinking, the Governor started to brag to his brother, "I built an amazingly beautiful inn on my property. It's not very far from here. You must go over and see it before you leave."

"Who runs the inn?" inquired the brother.

"Moshke, one of my Jews, runs the inn," answered the Governor.

"Those Jews again," retorted the brother, "they run everything. I can't stand them."

"Brother, please don't speak that way. The Jews manage everything on my estates and they do a very good job," said the Governor.

Just then, someone came to see the Governor on official business. The brother asked, "Since you'll probably be busy for awhile, could I borrow one of your horses and ride over to look at your inn?"

The governor was happy that his brother was going to see his pride and joy. "Quick," he ordered one of his servants, "saddle up my finest horse for my brother and give him exact directions to the inn."

Since the inn was located near the Governor's mansion, the brother rode off without a warm coat. After riding for some time, a light snow began to fall. Soon, the light snow fall turned into a heavy snowstorm. The brother got lost and rode for several more hours in the snow before arriving at the inn, nearly blue from the cold. Relieved that he had finally arrived at the inn, he jumped off his horse and tried to open the door. But it was locked. He could see people in the inn through the windows, so he started to knock with all his might on the door.

The innkeeper yelled through the door, "I'm sorry but I can't open the door because Rabbi Yisrael Baal Shem Tov is here."

The Governor's brother started to plead with him, "Please open the door, can't you see it's snowing and I'm freezing to death."

But the innkeeper answered, "I can't let you in because the Rabbi said to keep the doors and windows locked."

The Governor's brother started to pound frantically on the door with his fist while yelling to let him in.

Finally, the Baal Shem Tov motioned the innkeeper to open the door.

The governor's brother burst into the inn and rushed over to the hot oven to thaw out his nearly frozen hands and feet. When he finally warmed up, he asked: "Who is this Rabbi Yisrael Baal Shem Tov?" The innkeeper and his wife pointed towards the Baal Shem Tov.

The brother looked at the Baal Shem Tov who was still reading and not paying the slightest bit of attention to him. This disregard by the Baal Shem Tov made the Governor's brother more and more angry as he walked back and forth across the room, all the while glaring at the Baal Shem Tov. "Who is this Rabbi Baal Shem Tov," the Governor's brother screamed at the innkeeper, "that you did not open the door for me until I almost died of the cold?!"

The innkeeper and his wife meekishly pointed towards the Baal Shem Tov again.

Then the Governor's brother was overwhelmed with anger. He drew his sword and shouted at the Baal Shem Tov, "Prepare to die you fool!" Then he rushed towards the Baal Shem with his upraised sword.

At that very moment, the Baal Shem Tov yelled at the paralyzed woman, "Lift up both your hands!"

She raised her paralyzed hands and the Baal Shem Tov made a transference. The hands of the woman were restored to their former health, and the Governor's brother stopped in his tracks. The sword fell out of his hand. He could no longer move his hands or fingers and he could see his hands begin to wither away before his eyes.

"Please help me Rabbi," he screamed, "I'll do anything. I'm sorry. Please forgive me. My hands are paralyzed. My fingers won't move. Help me. I beg of you."

The Baal Shem Tov answered, "I cannot help you. The transference has occurred and it cannot be reversed."

When the couple returned to Mezibush, everyone crowded around to ask what happened. All the woman could say was "Baruch Hashem"[1] and then she wiggled her fingers to everyone's delight.

And so it was.

---

[1] Thank G•d.

CHAPTER EIGHT

NITZAVIM

"Today you are all standing before G•d, your G•d. . . . . even your woodcutters and water carriers . . . ."
Nitzavim 29:9,10

THE ZOLOTCHOVER WATER CARRIER

BEFORE leaving Mezibush, Reb Yechiel Michel of Zolotchov had yechidus with his Rebbe, the Holy Baal Shem Tov. During the yechidus, he requested, "Rebbe, please give me a blessing that I strengthen my service to HaShem."

The Baal Shem Tov gave him a blessing and then suggested that he visit the water carrier of Zolotchov on his way home and to give him the Baal Shem Tov's warmest regards. Of course, Reb Yechiel Michel was happy to carry out the Baal Shem Tov's simple request. As he was traveling to Zolotchov, he started thinking, "The water carrier can't be just a simple Jew.[1] If the Baal Shem Tov is sending me out of my way to see him and give him the Rebbe's regards, he must be a Tzaddik nistor."[2]

---

[1] A water carrier was typically one of the poorest Jews in the shtetl whose job it was to keep a wooden barrel in front of every house full, irrespective of the weather.
[2] Hidden holy man.

As soon as Reb Michel arrived in Zolotchov, he found where the water carrier lived and went directly to his house.

When the water carrier's wife came to the door, Reb Michel introduced himself and said, "I have regards for your husband from the Baal Shem Tov." He explained that he was returning home from a visit with the Rebbe and that the Rebbe had asked him to stop in Zolotchov and to convey his warm wishes to her husband, the Zolotchover water carrier.

"He is not home right now, but he will come shortly," the water carrier's wife answered. "You look tired from your travels," she continued, "won't you please come in and sit down and I'll get you a cold drink."

Reb Michel came into the water carrier's house. After he had a moment to look around, he thought, "My G•d, this is the most rundown house I've ever been in. There's almost no furniture and look at the children, they're so thin and barely dressed in rags."

A little while later, the Zolotchover water carrier arrived. He was overjoyed to receive the greeting from the Baal Shem Tov that his visitor, Reb Michel, conveyed. The water carrier immediately turned to his wife and said, "Please prepare a special meal for our guest. This is a special occasion for us. It's not every day that one receives regards from the Holy Baal Shem Tov."

The wife got busy preparing the feast, while Reb Michel told the water carrier some of the Torah teachings that the Baal Shem Tov had spoken while he was in Mezibush.

After some time, the wife called Reb Michel and her husband to the table for dinner. When they were seated, she served two small rolls and a dish of two tiny fish, one for each.

Before Reb Michel took the first bite, he heard the children whispering to each other, "He'll probably leave something for us. After all, a guest is not supposed to eat everything. Umm, that fish will be a real treat." Reb Michel felt so sorry for the children, he could barely get himself to even take the first bite. Then he thought, "These poor children, this poor family, what a way to live." He felt so bad that he could not keep from crying.

"Why are you weeping?" the water carrier asked his guest.

"I feel so sorry that you and your family have to suffer such poverty," answered Reb Michel.

"It's really not how it looks," answered the Zolotchover water carrier. "Let me explain with this parable."

A rich man, who was marrying off his daughter, invited all the local townspeople to the chasana. Being rich, the father spared no expense in the preparations. Everyone, and especially the poor people, eagerly awaited the day of the chasana. When the wedding day arrived, all of the townspeople gathered to partake in the Simcha and the dinner and dancing that followed the chupah. But just as the kallah was being led by her parents to the chupah, she fell down and fainted. After efforts to revive her were unsuccessful, the saddened wedding guests began leaving.

Meanwhile, some of the poor people who had been awaiting the wedding party for weeks, sat down at the food ladened tables and began eating. They said among themselves, "Of course we feel sorry for our host and the family, but why should all this food go to waste."

The other poor people, who also had been looking forward to a big, delicious meal didn't join their friends because they felt, "It just doesn't seem right to sit down and eat while our host is suffering."

"And this is how I look at my life," the Zolotchover water carrier explained. "The chasana represents the Beis Hamikdosh where all the Israelites gathered, at least three times a year, to rejoice with their host Hashem. And I am the type of poor soul who is sensitive to the Ribono Shel Olam's[1] misfortune, the destruction of the Beis Hamikdosh.[2] So I cannot bring myself to enjoy the bounty of this physical world while I know that the Ribono Shel Olam is still mourning the destruction of the Beis Hamikdosh and the exile of His people."

And so it was.

---

[1] Lord of the Universe.
[2] 70 C.E.

Today you are all standing firmly before G•d, your G•d. . . . even your wood cutters and water carriers. . . . " *Nitzavim 29:10*

Woodcutters and water drawers refer to the simple, unlearned Jews. *Divrei Chassidim*

IMPERFECT TRUTH AND PERFECT FAITH

THE Baal Shem Tov was known to be particularly fond of simple, G•d fearing Jews, and they in turn were his strongest supporters. Some of his closest disciples, who were typically great Torah scholars, could not understand their Rebbe's fondness for these unlearned people. Even more, they could not appreciate when the Baal Shem Tov sent them to learn traits, such as unquestioning trust and simple faith in G•d, and the love of a fellow Jew from such "ignorant" people.

The custom of the Baal Shem Tov was that the guests, who came to Mezibush for the Shabbos, joined him at the Friday night tish[1] and again the next day at the Third Meal during the twilight hours of the Shabbos afternoon. The midday Shabbos meal was set aside for the inner circle —

---

[1] A Chassidic gathering of Chassidim around their Rebbe.

the "Chevraya Kadisha" — the Holy Brotherhood — of learned disciples of the Baal Shem Tov.

One Shabbos, a group of visitors, all simple Jews such as innkeepers, bakers, butchers, candle stick makers, woodcutters, water drawers and the like, were at the shule of the Baal Shem Tov. The Baal Shem Tov, as was his custom, showed special attention to these simple people, by inviting them to his Friday night Shabbos tish at the shule. There he shared with them the Kiddush wine over which he sanctified the Shabbos; pieces of challah over which he had made a blessing; small pieces of meat and fish from his plate; and to another he even gave his own Kiddush cup to recite Kiddush.

The next day, the visitors ate the midday Shabbos meal at their lodgings, and then returned to the Baal Shem Tov's shule where they poured out their hearts in singing the praises and requests of the Book of Psalms.

After the Baal Shem Tov took his place at the head of the long table for the midday Shabbos meal, he indicated where each of the disciples in the Chevraya Kadisha should sit. At the conclusion of the meal, he revealed secrets from the Torah that caused the disciple's hearts to fill with spiritual delight. The disciples thanked their Heavenly

Father for bringing them into his spiritual
influence.

But the hearts of a few disciples were clouded
by judgment. "Why did the Rebbe show such favor
to followers that could not even understand his
teachings?" they thought.

At once, the face of the Baal Shem Tov
became very serious. In a quiet voice and with eyes
closed, he said: "Our sages teach, in a place where
a Baal Teshuvah stands, the most righteous man
has no place. There are two paths in the service of
the Creator — the first path is the righteous service
of the Tzaddik, and the second path is the contrite
service of the Baal Teshuvah. The service of
ordinary people belongs to the second path, the
level of the penitent — for they are of low spirit,
regretting their imperfect past, and striving to
improve their future conduct."

A quiet niggun began around the Shabbos
table, and those disciples who had doubts as to the
Rebbe's conduct realized that he sensed their
thoughts. Soon the niggun faded away and the Baal
Shem Tov opened his eyes and looked deeply into
the eyes of his disciples, one by one. Then he told
them to rest their right hand on the shoulder of
their neighbor and start another niggun. After they
had sung quietly for some time, he asked them to

close their eyes. He then rested his right hand on the shoulder of the disciple who was seated at his right, and his left hand on the shoulder of the disciple seated at his left. The circle was closed.

From that moment, the disciples heard the sweetest of melodies that carried the heartfelt requests of souls with them. 'Ribono Shel Olam!' said one voice, appealing to the Maker of the Universe in his own words, before going on to address Him in words used by King David in the Psalms: "Examine me, Oh G•d, and test me; refine my heart."

"Tayreh Tateh!"[1] another voice stated before saying the verse from Psalms. "Be gracious to me, Oh G•d, be gracious, for my soul trusts in You; and in the shadow of Your wings will I take refuge."

"Father!" came another cry, "even the sparrow has found a nest for herself. . . ."

The Holy Brotherhood of learned Chassidim trembled as they heard these innocent prayers. They shed tears from their closed eyes and envied the worship of these simple singers of Psalms.

The Baal Shem Tov lifted his hands from the shoulders of the disciples, and the music disappeared from their ears. He instructed them to

---

[1] Beloved father in Yiddish.

open their eyes, and to again sing a number of niggun together.

One of those present at that Shabbos table was Reb Dov Ber, later known as the Mezritcher Maggid and the next leader of the Chassidic movement following the Baal Shem Tov. Years later he recounted the incident to his disciple, Reb Schneur Zalman of Liadi, and told him at that moment he experienced a more intense love of the Creator than he had ever before known.

When the singing had come to an end, the brotherhood remained silent and the Baal Shem Tov sat with his eyes closed in a trance of dveikus. Then he looked up at his Chassidim and said: "The singing that you heard was the singing of verses from the Psalms from the bottom of the hearts of the simple people.

"Think of this: We are each a body, which is not a thing of truth, and a soul, which is truth — and even at that, the soul is only part of the Whole. Being imperfect truth, we are called 'sfas emes' (the lips of truth) — a mere hint of truth. Nevertheless, even when we are able to recognize and sense truth, we are overwhelmed by it. The Almighty treasures the humble words and blind faith of the Psalms of these simple people, whose praise transcends their limited understanding."

"For a long time thereafter," the Mezritcher Maggid told Reb Schneur Zalman, "I was distressed about my doubts as to the Rebbe's closeness with simple people. I undertook various fasts to rid myself of this past guilt, but could find no rest."

"Then one night, I saw a vision in a dream that brought peace to my soul. In one of the Heavenly palaces in the Garden of Eden, a group of young children were sitting around a table learning Chumash. At the head of the table sat their teacher — Moshe Rabbeinu. The children were studying the passage that speaks of the seeming disbelief of the Patriarch Avraham when he was given the Divine promise that in their old age, he and his wife would have a child. One of the children read aloud the verse in the Midrash: 'And Avraham fell on his face, and laughed and said in his heart, shall a child be born to one that is a hundred years old?'

"Moshe explained: How could our forefather Avraham possibly doubt that the Almighty could give a child to a hundred year old man? Because even the loftiest of souls exists within the natural order of the world, and within a simple human body."

When the Maggid heard that by simply existing within a physical body a person could experience doubts that arise of themselves, he was no longer troubled by his earlier misgivings about the Rebbe's conduct. At long last, his soul was at rest.

And so it was.

CHAPTER NINE

VAYEILECH

"The time is now approaching for you to die."
Vayeilech 31:14

THE PASSING

FOLLOWING the revelation of Rabbi Yisrael Ben Eliezer, the Baal Shem Tov, as a great Jewish leader and mystic, many of the Jewish community, especially in Poland, became his followers and students of the Chassidic path of Judaism. The time arrived all too soon for the Baal Shem Tov's passing to the next world.

For the Passover of 1760, Reb Pinchas of Koretz, came to visit his Rebbe, the Baal Shem Tov. On the afternoon before the seventh day of Passover began, Reb Pinchas was feeling weak and decided not to go to the mikveh as was his custom. The next day during his morning prayers, he had a premonition that the Baal Shem Tov would soon pass away. Reb Pinchas began to daven more intensely, begging that the Heavenly decree against the Baal Shem Tov be lifted. But he felt that he was unable to affect the decree and started to deeply regret that he had not gone to the mikveh the previous morning.

Coincidently, after morning prayers, the Baal Shem Tov asked Reb Pinchas if he had gone to the mikveh on the previous day. When he answered he had not, the Baal Shem Tov replied, "It's too late to correct that now."

After Passover, the Baal Shem Tov fell ill. However, he did not tell his followers and continued to pray before the Ark. While he might have told his close followers who were able to effect changes with their prayers in his physical condition, he sent them on missions to other communities. Reb Pinchas, knowing of the Heavenly decree against the Baal Shem Tov, did not return to his home but stayed with the Baal Shem Tov.

On the evening of Shavuos, many of the followers of the Baal Shem Tov gathered with him to spend the night learning Torah, as is the custom. The Baal Shem Tov expounded on the Torah portion of the week and the meaning of Shavuos.

In the morning, he sent for his closest followers and had them gather in his bed room. He told Reb Leib Kessler and several others to arrange for his burial. Because they were members of the funeral society and were knowledgeable about signs of illness, he showed them the signs on his body and explained how the soul emanates from each part.

Then, he told them to gather a minyan to pray with him. Before they began, he said, "Soon I shall be with the Holy One, blessed be He."

After the prayers, Reb Nachman of Horodenka went to the beis medrash to pray for the Baal Shem Tov. Later, the Baal Shem Tov said, "He petitions in vain. Maybe if he could have entered in the Heavenly gate where I was accustomed to enter, his prayers would have helped."

At that moment, the soul of a dead man came to the Baal Shem Tov asking for redemption. The Baal Shem Tov rebuked him, saying: "For eighty years you have wandered, and you have not bothered to come until the day of my parting from this world. Go away you rasha."

Immediately afterwards, the Baal Shem explained to his gabbai what had just happened and then instructed him, "Go quickly and tell everyone to stay away from the road because I angered that soul and he may hurt someone." But unfortunately, before the gabbai had a chance to warn everyone, the soul had already injured a girl, the daughter of the gabbai.

When the gabbai returned to report what happened, he heard the Baal Shem Tov say, "I grant you these two hours. Do not torture me."

The gabbai asked, "Rebbe, who are you talking to?"

The Baal Shem Tov answered, "Don't you see the Angel of Death? Before, he always ran from me. As people said, 'I banished him to where black peppers grow.' Now that he has been given control over me, he stands straighter and laughs at me."

In the early afternoon, shortly after morning prayers, the town's people who did not know of the Baal Shem Tov's condition came to see him. As always, he delivered a discourse of Torah to them. Later, during the Yom Tov meal, he asked his gabbai to put mead in a large glass. Instead, the gabbai put the mead in a small glass.

The Baal Shem Tov quipped, "Man has no power on the day of death; even the gabbai does not obey me." Then he said to the gabbai, "Until now I have done favors for you. Now please do a favor for me and give me a large glass of mead."

All of the close disciples were sitting in the room of the Baal Shem Tov while he lay in his bed. He gave them a sign. "My friends, when I leave this world, both clocks in this room will stop." His followers saw the hands of the big clock stop while he washed his hands. They stood in front of the clock so that the Baal Shem wouldn't see that the clock had stopped. He said to them, "My friends, I am not concerned for myself because I know that when I leave through the door of this world, I'll immediately enter into the door of the next world."

The Baal Shem Tov then sat up in his bed and told them to gather around him. He expounded Torah about the column on which one ascends from lower paradise to upper paradise, and how this was so in each of the four worlds. Then he described the world of the souls, and the order of worship. He instructed them to say with him, "Let the pleasantness of the L•rd our G•d be upon us." He lay down and sat up several times. Meanwhile he concentrated on mystical kavanahs until they could not distinguish the syllables of his speech.

Finally he lay down and told them to cover him with a sheet. The Baal Shem Tov began to tremble as when he said the eighteen benedictions. Slowly he became quiet and the followers saw that the small clock had stopped. They waited for a long time but he didn't move. After that, they put a feather under his nose to detect his breathing and realized that he had passed away.

Rabbi Jacob of the holy community of Mezibush, reported that Reb Leib Kessler told him that he saw the departure of his soul as a blue flame.

And so it was.

"The time is now approaching for you to die."
Vayeilech 31:14

FEIVISH LOWEST OF THE LOW

IN the holy sefer, "Toldos Yaakov", a woman
from the community of Mezibush is quoted as
having said: "The Jewish people have done well to
have chosen G•d as their L•rd, but Hashem too has
selected well by choosing Israel as His nation, for
even the lowly Feivish consecrated His holy name."

Reb Nachman Kahana, the Spinker Rebbe in
Bnei Brak, explained her words with the following
story:

There once lived in the vicinity of Mezibush a
fabulously wealthy man who had an only daughter.
When the time came for her to be married, her
father approached a local rosh yeshiva in search of
a likely candidate. The rosh yeshiva suggested Reb
Feivish, a gifted young student with a brilliant mind
and equally admirable character traits.

The wealthy man, a learned man himself,
spoke with the young man and was so impressed
that he immediately asked the rosh yeshiva to
propose the match to the young Feivish. To further
entice Reb Feivel, the father guaranteed a

substantial dowry and promised to support his son-in-law for the rest of his days so that he might be free to pursue the study of Torah.

It goes without saying that Feivish was pleased with these conditions and agreed to the match.

The wedding took place after several months and the young couple went to live next door to her parent's home. Feivish continued studying Torah while his father-in-law continued to manage his business, providing for the young couple as he had promised. To the wealthy man's delight, Feivish, being clever and sharp, found favor among the townspeople and they began coming to him with their various problems.

Many years passed and two daughters were born to Feivish and his wife.

The years claimed their toll on the rich man and he felt that he could no longer carry the burden of his business upon his shoulder.

One day, while discussing the future with his wife, she offered this suggestion: "My husband, you are already old. You cannot continue devoting the same attention to your business as in the past for you simply do not have the strength. Is it not true that your laborers take advantage of you and try to cheat you at every occasion? You simply cannot continue this way indefinitely. You have children and grandchildren to support, and we too, must be provided for in our old age. I suggest that you take our son-in-law into the business. Let him start with an hour a day until he gets acquainted with all its workings. He is a clever man and will eventually be able to considerably lighten your burden. And besides, he will eventually have to take over the business when, after 120 years, you depart from this world."

The man listened to his wife's words but thoroughly disagreed. "It is not fair to Feivish," he argued. "He agreed to marry our daughter on the condition that he would not be required to concern himself with business matters. It would be totally unfair to involve him in worldly affairs when he is so diligent and devoted to his study. That is, after all, much more important." The controversy raged back and forth.

One day the daughter entered her parent's home to find her mother sitting and sobbing.

"Whatever is the matter, Mother? Is everyone well? What is wrong?"

The mother explained her feelings, describing her concern for the future of the family. She reviewed all her arguments while her daughter listened.

"But Mother," the daughter finally said, "you know that Feivish studies day and night, never wasting a minute. When could he possibly learn the business?"

The mother responded, "He doesn't have to assume complete responsibility at once. Let him but put in an hour a day to acquaint himself with the business."

The daughter, seeing her mother's deep concern in the matter, promised to speak to Feivish about it. The following day, when Feivish returned from the beis medrash, his wife greeted him despondently. Concerned, he asked her why she seemed so troubled. She told him of her conversation with her mother and begged him to begin taking an interest in her father's business, if only for an hour a day. At first Feivish was strongly opposed, but the power of the evil inclination is so mighty that he finally agreed.

Feivish began going to the store for an hour a day, but even during this hour, he would immerse himself in a sefer and study all the while.

The Satan was not satisfied with the state of things and laid further plans to tear Feivish away from Torah study.

"You scoundrel! You dirty thief!" were the words that Feivish heard one day as he sat in the store pouring over a sefer. An angry merchant had burst into the store and was now accusing his father-in-law of dishonest dealings.

". . . . and don't think that this is the first time you've cheated me! I pay you in full each time for all the merchandise that I order and then you go ahead and swindle me in the amount that you deliver!" accused the enraged customer.

The father-in-law opened the package thrust before him on the counter and saw that his customer's accusation was quite valid. He cross-examined his workers until he found the culprit who had been stealing the merchandise. He settled the matter with his disgruntled customer and fired his dishonest worker.

This scene had its effect on Feivish. He realized that the workers took advantage of his father-in-law, stealing whenever his back was turned. He decided that it was up to him to take a more active interest in the business to prevent such unpleasant scenes in the future. Feivish started coming for two or three hours daily, becoming engrossed with the comings and goings of the laborers and customers. His father-in-law, relieved to shed some of his responsibility, relied more and more on Feivish as he saw the capable young man grasp all the facets of the business.

Feivish, seeing that the present laborers could not be trusted, dismissed all of them and hired others to replace them, reorganizing the whole business.

Thus it happened that when the father-in-law passed away, Feivish was left totally involved in financial affairs. Satan had won the first round.

By now, Feivish was spending the whole day at the store. This left him virtually no time for Torah study. He set aside an hour in the mornings before prayers and another in the evenings, but the business soon encroached even upon these precious hours. He found that during business hours he had to tend to customers so that he was required to review his accounts in the evening.

Since Feivish stayed up till late at night over his accounts, he was too tired in the mornings to adhere to his schedule of one hour of study. His morning prayers became increasingly hurried until he stopped davening with a minyan altogether.

The business prospered and Feivish soon found it necessary to expand. This naturally meant more responsibility and less free time. When Feivish was appointed as an official supplier of the Russian King, the added burden left him with no time even for his prayers. On Shabbos, he still managed to daven in a synagogue. But soon he stopped this too, being so worn out from his strenuous efforts of the week. He would spend the whole day in bed, just recovering his strength for the week to come. Satan had won again.

His position as official supplier to the King once presented an excellent business opportunity to Feivish. He was invited to the prime minister's home to sign a contract on a large order. Since he felt it unseemly to appear as he was, he trimmed his beard, acquired different clothing, and went to keep his appointment. As he sat discussing business, the prime minister's wife entered with refreshments. Feivish did not wish to insult his hostess and tasted one of the cakes laid before him. By way of compliment, he casually asked her what they were made of, and was relieved to hear that they contained no treife (non-kosher) ingredients. And thereafter, when his affairs brought him to the prime minister's home again, he would partake of the refreshments without pangs of conscience. Little did he realize that the woman did, in fact, use lard and fats to enhance the flavor of her baked foods.

Once he had become lax in his eating habits, he felt no compunctions about eating treife, eventually bringing such food into his own home.

His wife, distressed by Feivish's downfall, was powerless to do anything. It pained and grieved her deeply to see the metamorphosis of her husband from a Torah scholar to an unobservant Jew, but she no longer had any influence upon him and was forced to remain silent. His G•dless ways were apparent to the whole community and Feivish acquired the name, "Feivish, Lowest of the Low".

The years passed and Feivish continue to prosper. The time arrived for him to marry off his older daughter. Although he realized that he was a sinner, Feivish desired the best for his daughter, a Torah scholar and an upright young man. But no one who knew Feivish or had even heard of him would be likely to consent to become his son-in-law. He decided to take a business trip, combining it with a search for a suitable young man. He took along with him his tallis and tefillin, though he had long ceased using them.

His travels brought Feivish to Hungary where he stopped at a village. When he entered the synagogue, he encountered a fine young student, whose very face bespoke his greatness. Upon inquiry, he learned that he was the son of the local rabbi who was also head of the Beis Din — the rabbinical court. After talking with the youth and becoming enamored of his fine qualities, Feivish desired him as a son-in-law.

Feivish returned home and summoned a penniless shadchan (matchmaker). He offered him a substantial sum to go to the village in Hungary and transact the shiduch[1] with the young man he had previously met. The shadchan accepted the project and immediately set forth.

When the shadchan reached the village, he went straight to the rabbi's home. Posing as a grain merchant, he said that business had brought him to Hungary where he was required to remain for several weeks. Since he was very particular in observance of kashrus, he begged the rabbi to accept him as a paying guest. The rabbi, who barely subsisted upon his meager salary, agreed to the arrangement. The shadchan made himself very amenable during his stay. He possessed a glib tongue and would entertain the whole household with his amusing and interesting anecdotes.

One day he approached the rabbi with a suggestion. "I see that your son has already reached marriageable age."

"Yes, that is true," replied the rabbi. "Indeed, he has had many offers for a shiduch, but they all

---

[1] Match for marriage.

require that we put up a large sum of money, which in our circumstances, we cannot possibly afford."

"Then I have just the thing for you," answered the Shadchan. "You see, before I left my home town I was approached by a Talmud Chacham, a man expert in Shas and the Poskim, who is also extremely wealthy to the bargain. He told me that he sought for his accomplished daughter, a fine youth who would be willing to spend the rest of his days in Torah study. If I were to come across such a youth, I should feel free to represent him and suggest the match."

After having lived here for a while, I feel I know you both, the honorable father and the learned son, well enough to feel that something might come of my humble suggestion."

The rabbi listened to his guest's words and agreed to meet with the father. The shadchan immediately wrote to Feivish that the rabbi was amenable and that he was to come and make his acquaintance.

Feivish's trip took several weeks but when he arrived he was loaded with expensive gifts for the entire family. Although his outward appearance did not make the most favorable impression, the rebbetzyn assumed that this wealthy businessman certainly came in contact with high officials and must alter his appearance for their sake. But when the rabbi spoke to Feivish, he was truly amazed at his erudition in Torah knowledge.

The couple now desired to see the daughter, but Feivish convinced them to first announce the engagement. If his daughter did not meet up with their expectations when she came with him on his next business trip, the engagement would automatically be declared void.

A feast was made to celebrate the joyous occasion. Many poor people were invited and the chosson[1] delivered a brilliant speech. Feivish discussed several points, posing contradictions and resolving them with his vast knowledge. The chosson and his parents were very happy and eagerly awaited further developments.

Feivish took leave of his future mechutanim, again showering them with gifts. He promised to return soon with his daughter. When he did return with her, she was approved by the rabbi and his family. Feivish then suggested that they celebrate the wedding right away.

"Why must you be bothered by such a lengthy trip to our city? It is both tiring and expensive. And besides, how do you propose to leave your city without its leader? Let us celebrate

---

[1] Bridegroom.

the wedding here and now, and then I will take the young couple back with me to their new home."

The rabbi agreed and the wedding took place within the week. Hundreds of people attended from the choson's side but the kallah[1] and her father were the only ones to represent their side of the family. Feivish explained that they had few relations and that distance prevented their friends from attending.

After the seven days of celebration following the wedding, Feivish and the young couple packed their things and set out for home.

When they finally reached their destination, they were greeted by many servants who rushed to take in their things and make them comfortable. The young chosen was not accustomed to the splendor and wealth that was apparent all around him. They first entered a large courtyard of a mansion lit up by many lanterns, surrounded by orchards and gardens from whence emanated a mixture of Heavenly fragrances. The rugs and tapestries that adorned the rooms of the mansion stunned the youth who had never seen such wealth in all his days.

The chosson and kallah were taken to their room to refresh themselves. Just as they had made

---

[1] Bride.

themselves comfortable, a knock was heard at the door. It was Feivish, who begged to speak several words with his new son-in-law.

"I think it is only fair to inform you of certain things before you become a permanent member of my household. I am known in these parts as "Feivish, Lowest of the Low": this is because I transgress all the commandments of the Torah. I wish you to hear it first from me before you hear it from outsiders. You may accuse me of having deceived you but first let me state my case.

"Even though I myself am no longer an observant Jew, I desire a pious and scholarly husband for my daughter. I will give you your own home complete with new furniture and dishes and you need have no contact with me at all. I agree to continue to support you for the rest of your days. If however, you still wish to back out, you must give your wife a divorce immediately and renounce all claims against me. Furthermore, you may keep all the gifts I have given to you until now. But whatever you decide. I want that decision to be made by morning."

The poor young man was thoroughly shaken up. What a disgrace for his eminent father and for himself as well, to be thus connected with a man known as "The Lowest of the Low"! His decision was clear; he would divorce his wife the very next day and return home.

But when he had time to reflect longer, his mind was filled with conflicting thoughts.

"Does it not say: 'He who divorces his first wife - the very altar sheds tears for him.' How can I return home and tell everyone that my father-in-law is an unobservant Jew? Who will believe me after the wonderful impression he made upon my whole village? They will all whisper that it is all my fault that the marriage did not succeed. And it won't be easy for me to find myself another wife after this."

Opposing arguments now rushed into his mind. "Perhaps this is a plot fostered by the evil inclination to ruin me. Just as my father-in-law was seduced into abandoning the tenets of Judaism, so might I be led astray."

Suddenly he was reminded of his new wife. "Why must she be punished for her father's sins? She was a good woman and had every right to live a Torah-true life."

He confronted his wife with this question: "Would you then be satisfied with leading a Torah life in contrast to the life you have led under your father's roof?"

"My dear husband," said the young woman earnestly, tears streaming down her cheeks, "do you not realize that it is not you alone that I married, but all that you stand for? How I have hated this life I lead here! How I have yearned to live a Torah life. Never fear — I will not hinder you from your studies but will do all in my power to encourage you and help you."

The entire night passed while the young man considered and weighed all aspects of his situation. Early the next morning, a knock was again heard at the door. The chosson told the waiting Feivish that he had decided to remain. Feivish then took his son-in-law and showed him his new lodgings and told him that he would have furniture delivered that very day. The young man then went to the beis medrash to daven.

The people there greeted the newcomer and, noticing his Hungarian manner of dress, asked if he had come to stay. The young man then explained that he had married Feivish's daughter. Everyone was shocked to hear this and hastened to warn him about his father-in-law's irreligious ways, lest he be influenced by them. He listened to their warnings politely and then went home to study.

Rebbe Baal Shem Tov lived not far from Feivish and the young son-in-law began to frequent the Rebbe's beis medrash. In a short time, he spent several days each week studying by the Baal Shem Tov and then returned home for Shabbos.

Two years passed and Feivish's second daughter became of a marriageable age. Feivish reasoned that his chances for getting a scholarly husband for her were even slimmer than before, for his first son-in-law had surely written home about him. He would now be notorious even in Hungary. He decided therefore to travel to a distant part in Russia and begin his search there.

After weeks of travel, he arrived at a small village and entered its beis medrash. There he found the rabbi, a follower of the Baal Shem Tov, seated at a table surrounded by his Chassidim, engrossed in Torah study. Impressed by the scene, Feivish made inquiries about this rabbi. When he learned that he had a son who was likewise a pious scholar, he was overjoyed. He hurried home and summoned the shadchan to him once again. This time however, the shadchan was loath to perform the deceptive mission and it required a doubling of the previous fee to persuade him.

The shadchan arrived at his destination and went to the beis medrash. The rabbi was again seated with his talmidim (students). The shadchan sat down and joined them at their study. Eventually he brought the talk around to the Baal Shem Tov, about whom he knew many fascinating stories. His audience listened to him spellbound, their admiration and affection towards the capable storyteller growing by the minute. When the shadchan felt that the Chassidim knew him well enough, he approached the rabbi's young son with his proposal for a shidach.

The young man listened respectfully, and then referred him to his mother. The rebbetzyn also listened with interest but told him that it was her husband, the rabbi, who made all such decisions. She finally agreed, after much pleading on the shadchan's part, to personally approach her husband about this matter. She relayed to the rabbi all the information that the shadchan had told her, of Feivish's wealth and of his scholarly son-in-law, the husband to Feivish's first daughter. The rabbi did indeed recall seeing the young man by the Baal Shem Tov but he refused to commit himself without first seeing Feivish.

The shadchan duly summoned Feivish to come and discuss the matter with the rabbi. But as soon as the rabbi beheld Feivish's face, he intuitively felt that it was the face of a sinner. Loath to discuss the matter, he asked Feivish to leave the next day.

That evening, the rabbi prayed that it be revealed to him in a dream what course of action he was to take. That very night he had a dream in which he was told that even though Feivish himself was a sinner, his daughter was the predestined wife for his son. The rabbi was not to do anything to prevent this match for it was Heaven ordained and would come to pass in any event. The rabbi immediately awoke and hurried to Feivish's room with his answer.

Feivish had been lying in bed when suddenly he heard footsteps coming towards his room. He hurriedly donned a robe, and went over to his table to pore over a Gemora, pretending that he had been studying all evening. The rabbi knocked and was told to enter.

"You have nothing to hide from me," the rabbi told his startled guest, "I know just what kind of a man you are and all your sins have been revealed to me. However, I agree to go through with the match for I have been informed that it is so willed in Heaven."

Feivish was relieved with this news, as well as by the fact that he need not maintain his pretenses any longer. He therefore decided to hold the wedding in his city. He set a date for the event and returned home.

Feivish's family was overjoyed to hear the good news and most of all the first son-in-law. He would now have a companion with whom he could study. It was he who made all the arrangements for the forthcoming wedding, making sure of course that all the food would be of the highest degree of kashrus.

The week of the wedding arrived. The rabbi, with his immediate family and talmidim arrived in the city before Shabbos. Their arrival made a big stir in the community, but when the townspeople learned that the visiting rebbe was to be Feivish's mechutan, they simply shook their heads in bewilderment. They tried to forewarn him of Feivish's true nature but the rabbi's mind was made up.

The wedding day arrived and all rejoiced — Feivish on having succeeded in again acquiring a scholarly son-in-law, the rabbi on having married off his son so painlessly, and the first son-in-law on having acquired a pious brother-in-law.

During the festivities, the rabbi stood up and proposed a toast. "To your true repentance, mechutan."

"No, rabbi." answered Reb Feivish, "I'm afraid the time has not arrived as yet."

"When then will you repent?"

"Ah, if only I knew when I was to die, I would repent three days before my death."

"Let me have your promise on that," said the rabbi, and he leaned over to grasp Feivish's hand firmly. The week of festivities over, the rabbi returned home with his talmidim and the new husband assumed his responsibilities. Feivish provided a home complete with new furnishings and utensils for the couple, and life settled down to normal. The two brothers-in-law now went together to the Baal Shem Tov where they studied and received spiritual guidance.

The years passed and the rabbi, the father of his second son-in-law, departed from this world but Feivish lived on, steeped in his evil ways. One Shabbos night, he returned home from a wild party he had attended and threw himself down upon his bed. Suddenly the door of his chamber opened slowly and a man dressed all in white entered. It was Feivish's mechutan, the rabbi.

"I have come from Heaven to remind you of the promise you made at your daughter's wedding. In three days time you will die. The time has come for you to repent for your wicked ways."

The rabbi disappeared as silently as he had come. Feivish sat up in bed all shaken. "Is it possible to repent in three days time," he wondered, "for what I have transgressed during these last thirty years?"

Suddenly he fell into a fit. He screamed and struck his head against the wall and no one could restrain him. A doctor was quickly summoned but Feivish did not let him get near. Finally, the two sons-in-law were called. When they appeared, Feivish calmed down somewhat and told them what had happened.

"What am I to do? How can I possibly repent all my sins? Maybe you can take me to the Baal Shem Tov? Right now! If anyone can still help me, it is he."

The two young men immediately ordered the carriage prepared and were soon speeding towards Mezibush, the town where the Baal Shem Tov lived.

It was already after midnight and their only concern was how to get in to see the holy Baal Shem Tov at this late hour. But as soon as they arrived, the shammos who had been instructed by the Baal Shem Tov to immediately bring Reb Feivish in, hurried out to them and asked: "Has Reb Feivish arrived?"

Upon entering the Baal Shem Tov's study, Feivish threw himself down at the Rebbe's feet and burst into uncontrollable sobbing, his life's story emerging between his racking cries.

"You can still repent, Feivish," said the Rebbe. "Now listen. You must fast for the next three days and spend the entire time in the beis medrash in prayer and repentance. When the people come to pray in the morning and evening, you are to throw yourself down at their feet and exclaim, 'I am Feivish the Sinner who has transgressed all the commandments of the Torah. I regret it all and have accepted upon myself the burden of repentance as specified by the Baal Shem Tov.' In addition to this, you are to throw yourself down at the feet of anyone who enters the beis medrash during the day and repeat what I have just told you."

"Is that all, Rebbe? How can these actions atone for thirty years of heavy sinning?"

"You just do as I have instructed and all will turn out well."

Feivish set out immediately for the beis medrash to begin his program of Teshuvah. He recited Tehillim all day and night, he confessed his sins before everyone who entered the beis medrash, and he wept and fasted all the while. By the third day he was at the end of his strength.

These developments irked and inflamed the Satan. The man whom he had ensnared in his nets for thirty years was now making amends for them in three days time! It was just not fair! All of his work was being nullified. He raised a riot in Heaven at the injustice of such instant teshuvah and the Heavenly Court ruled that the Satan might descend to have another try at corrupting Reb Feivish. If Satan could succeed in forcing Reb Feivish to taste a bit of treife food again, his repentance would not be accepted.

On Tuesday afternoon, a distinguished person entered the beis medrash. Feivish rushed over, and throwing himself down at his feet, made his usual confession.

"What kind of silly behavior is this for a grown man?" asked the stranger.

Feivish explained his situation and said that the Baal Shem Tov had instructed him to thus prostrate himself at every newcomer's feet. The man sat himself at a table and opened a Gemora. He began learning out loud, pretending that he could barely understand the text. Feivish politely interrupted him.

"Please forgive my impertinence," said Reb Feivel, "but that is not the way one should understand that particular passage."

"If you are indeed a learned man, then why must you abase yourself in such a manner? Does it not say that if a scholar sins let him study two pages of Gemora and he will be strengthened by Torah?"

Meanwhile a minyan had gathered in the beis medrash to daven mincha. Feivish, greatly weakened by his three-day fast, struggled to stand up and go over to them, but the stranger tried to detain him.

"Does it not also say, 'And you shall guard your lives exceedingly.' If you continue fasting any longer you may not last the day. How then will you propose to repent the sin of suicide on top of all your other transgressions?"

Feivish hurried nevertheless to fulfill the Baal Shem Tov's instructions and threw himself down before the men who had assembled. Then he returned to the stranger who had meanwhile taken out a package of food.

Feivish was literally dying for just a taste of fresh bread. The stranger offered to share his meal. Feivish wavered. Suddenly he noticed that a drop of candle wax, which was made from animal fats, had fallen into the stranger's soup.

"I wouldn't touch that soup, its treife!" he shouted. The stranger then tried to make him taste some challah. But since Feivish had not washed his hands and said the required blessing, he refused to eat the bread.

"Here you are on the very threshold of starvation and you still stand on ceremony? Come with me," said the stranger, "I will help you wash your hands."

The stranger took Feivish to the sink but for some unknown reason, there was no water in the faucets. He then led the weakened but resisting Feivish to the mikveh where there was sure to be water. But here too there was no water, the mikveh was empty. The man was disappointed. Poor Feivish summoned up his last ounce of strength to wrench himself away from his persuasive captor and jumped head first into the empty mikveh. As he was falling, he felt the Baal Shem Tov's holy hands on him and he heard his voice.

"Feivish, it was such a self-sacrifice that we had hoped of you. Now all your sins are atoned for. Rest now in peace."

It was concerning this Feivish that they said, "Feivish the Lowly sanctified G•d's holy name in public."

And so it was.

CHAPTER TEN

HA'AZINU

". . . . be careful to observe all the words of this Torah. For it is not an empty thing for you. Rather it is your life!" *Ha'azinu 32:46,47*

Statutes are commandments that have no logical reason. Laws are ethical commandments. Since we are to 'live' with them, we can also learn from this statement that we only keep the commandments when they don't endanger our life.

A NEW WAY OF SERVING

ONCE there was a heated discussion between a group of Torah scholars and the Baal Shem Tov. The Torah scholars, who were somewhat antagonistic to the teachings of the Baal Shem Tov, said, "Rabbi Yisrael, for many centuries it has been an established custom, supported by the Gemora and later mystical literature, for people trying to better serve G•d to fast. The purpose of fasting was to weaken the body and increase the power of the soul in the service of G•d. Often, people would even fast throughout the week and only eat on the Shabbos."

"We've heard that you instruct your followers to avoid fasting except during the fast days established and obligated by our Rabbis and according to Torah law. We've even heard that you claim that, 'someone that does extra fasts will later (in Heaven) be called upon to account for causing themselves physical suffering.' In fact, it is said that you've even gone so far as to say that 'extra fasting is a sin'."

The Baal Shem Tov explained, "I've come to introduce a new way of serving HaShem. There are three major principles is this new way of serving HaShem. They are love of G•d, love of a fellow Jew and love of Torah. In my opinion, there is no need for the self torment of fasting. The reason is that fasting has a tendency to cause melancholy and gloom. It is a well known principle that the Shechinah does not rest upon one who is sad but only rests upon one that is b'simchah[1] in their performance of a mitzvah."

"At this time before the coming of the Moshiach," the Baal Shem Tov went on to say, "there is usually no need for self torment. There is, however, a great need to be b'simcha. As King David said, 'Evdoo es HaShem b'simcha (Serve the L•rd with a joyful attitude) *Psalm 100:2*.' And with this way of serving HaShem, we can usher in the time of the Moshiach quickly in our days."

And so it was.

---

[1] Joyful.

"Through this thing, you will lengthen your days. . . . " *Ha'azinu 32:47*

THE HIDDEN TZADDIK

WHEN the fifth Lubavitcher Rebbe, Rabbi Shalom DovBer Schneerson (1860-1920) was a young child, his father (the fourth Lubavitcher Rebbe, Rebbe Shmuel) woke him one morning and asked him if he had dreamed anything. The boy thought for a minute, then began trembling with fear and answered that he dreamed that several awesomely holy men had visited him and that one of them told him a Torah teaching and a story.

He described them and his father identified the one who had spoken as Rabbi Yisrael Baal Shem Tov.

The Torah idea that the Baal Shem Tov said was:

It is written in *Ethics of the Fathers* (4:1): "Who is strong? He who conquers his selfish inclinations." It does not say "who *breaks* his selfish inclinations" but rather "who conquers...", True power lies in conquering and transforming one's selfish drives in order to use *them* to serve G•d as well as oneself.

146

The story that the Baal Shem Tov told was as follows:

When I was a young man of twenty, soon after being accepted as a member of the society the hidden Tzaddikim,[1] several of us came to the city of Brody.

It was there in Brody that I saw the most amazing thing. I was standing in the market place speaking to a large group of locals when I noticed from the corner of my eye an older man walking in the distance, bent under the burden of a large sack he was carrying on his shoulder. His face was covered with sweat and there was nothing unusual about him except for the fact that over his head floated a brilliant pillar of spiritual fire!

Obviously none of the other townspeople saw it. A few of them even yelled jeeringly, "Keep going Herschel Goat" and, "Carry, Herschel, carry!" And he called back with a smile, "Thank you! G•d bless you!"

I could not believe my eyes. I called two of the elder Tzaddikim, Rabbi Yechezkel and Rabbi Ephraim, who were with me. They too, saw the pillar of fire above man's head but also couldn't

---

[1] The "hidden Tzaddikim" were a group of unusually gifted and devoted Jews who, disguised as simple people, dedicated their lives to improving the plight of their Jewish brethren both spiritually and materially.

explain it. For all appearances, this Herschel was just an ordinary, poor Jewish man trying to make a living. I couldn't stop wondering what was the reason that he deserved such a great revelation?

For several days I observed him and tried to understand the reason for this holy fire, but I still had no idea. The local townspeople people told me that he was a widower, his wife having died some ten years before. He earned his meek living by carrying things on his back and doing odd jobs, and as far as everyone knew, he used all his money to feed a few goats he owned because he loved goat milk. That is how he earned the name "Herschel Goat".

So I decided to fast the first three days of each week, only drinking water at night, until I understood what this man did that was so pleasing to G•d.

I had just finished the first three days and was leaving the local shule when by Divine Providence, there was Herschel walking down the street. He had a big smile on his face as I approached him. I told him I was very weak from having fasted and asked if he could give me something to eat.

"Of course! Of course!" he said joyously. "Please, just follow me to my home! I'm so happy to help you."

We walked for about an hour till we came to an old run-down hut at the edge of the forest. Nothing seemed unusual until he opened the door and we entered.

Suddenly, four or five goats from all corners of the hut jumped at him. They lovingly licked his hands and literally pranced with joy about him.

I had never quite seen the like of it. Herschel quieted the goats, told me to sit down, took out a large metal pail, milked one of them, and poured me a cup to drink.

"Nothing's healthier than goat's milk! Here, have another," he said with satisfaction as he handed me a second cup.

When I tried to pay him he refused. "G•d forbid! Money? No! It's my pleasure! I'm the one that benefits! What, I should take money too?" he said with a smile on his face.

Then he looked at me seriously and said, "I want to tell you a true story. You have no idea how happy I am that you came here. Please listen." He sat down opposite me waited a few moments collecting his thoughts, and began.

"My wife of blessed memory was a truly righteous woman, always helping people. Any time anyone lacked anything, she was there doing everything she could to help. She collected money for charity and cared for people when they were sick; everything she did was for others. Shortly after she passed away, after the seven days of mourning, she appeared to me in a dream.

"She told me that after she died, instead of going through the painful and frightening spiritual purification processes of 'the slingshot' and 'the trashing of the grave,' she was received warmly by the souls of all those people she had helped and led directly to one of the highest Heavenly chambers.

"She told me that nothing is valued in Heaven more than brotherly love and beseeched me to also begin a life of charity and good deeds.

"That is why I bought these goats. I give free milk to whoever needs it and it has done wonders for people, simply wonders, and I am so happy I can help.

"Since then my wife never appeared to me again. It's been ten years since then, but today, just before I awoke this morning, she appeared in a dream. She told me that this morning I would meet a holy man and he would change my life, and I'm sure she was talking about you. Please stay with me for a few days and teach me Torah."

I stayed with Herschel for several days and watched the way he lovingly cared for his goats and how he dispensed their milk to dozens of people that needed it, everything done with a simple, contagious joy and with no egotism whatsoever. But on the other hand he was a simple, uneducated man and could barely read.

I discussed the matter with the Tzaddikim and we decided to take him under our wing and teach him Torah. For three years we taught him the most basic books and then one day his mind simply opened. He suddenly understood and remembered everything we taught him, even the most difficult concepts in Talmud and in Kabbalah, but he never lost his simplicity.

After five more years, he became a great hidden Tzaddik and mystic in his own right, moved to the city of Ostropol, and for the next ten years helped and even saved hundreds of Jews with his prayers and blessings.

But the story has a strange ending. As fate would have it, Herschel passed away on a cold rainy day. The burial society of Ostropol did provide ten Jews to escort him to his final resting place, but otherwise treated him like a simple pauper. This was not received well in Heaven. After all, Reb Herschel was a holy man and had helped myriads of people and deserved much more honorable treatment.

A decree was passed in the Heavenly Court that the city of Ostropol should suffer terrible misfortunes because of their mistreatment of Reb Herschel.

I and many others tried to avert the decree, but to no avail. It seems that disgracing a Tzaddik, although they do not care about their own honor, is no small matter.

Until suddenly, the soul of Herschel's wife appeared before the Heavenly Court.

All the accusing angels fell silent and she spoke. How could it be that the entire city of Ostropol would be punished because of her husband? Her husband had devoted his life to helping people. The greatest possible disgrace that could be done to him would be to cause anyone, no less an entire city, to suffer on his account. She demanded that the punishment be annulled.

"After short deliberation," the Baal Shem Tov concluded his tale, "her demands were met."

And so it was.

CHAPTER ELEVEN

VEZOS HABRACHAH

"And this is the blessing which Moshe, a man of G•d gave to the Children of Israel, (shortly) before his death." *Vezos Habrachah 33:1*

THE NIGGUN OF AROUSAL

AND then there was the time, just before the Baal Shem Tov passed on to the next world, that he gathered his closest followers around his death bed and asked them to sing the Hisorerus — Rachamim Rabim Niggun[1] of Reb Michel of Zlotchov.

Summoning all of his last strength, the Baal Shem Tov sat up in bed and announced: "I hereby guarantee you and all coming generations, that whenever someone sings this song of inspiration with a true desire to arouse himself to repentance, no matter where or who he is, I will come to join him in his song and help arouse Heavenly mercy for him."

And so it was.

---

[1] Tune of Spiritual Inspiration.

"So Moses, the servant of G•d died there . . . . . "
Vezos Haberachah 34:5

THE LAST REVELATION

ON the day of his passing from the world on the first day of Shavuot, the Baal Shem Tov was in his bed surrounded by his closest Chassidim. Only Reb Hershelah Tzvi, the Baal Shem Tov's son, was absent.

The Chassidim warily asked, "Rebbe, don't you want to give your son a few last instructions?"

The Baal Shem Tov answered with a sigh, "How can I? He is still sleeping."

A few Chassidim rushed out to wake Reb Hershelah. "Reb Hershelah, quick, wake up, your father the Rebbe is getting ready to leave the world."

"Oh no," answered Reb Hershelah with a shock, "That's impossible! I don't believe my father is passing on to the next world."

"Reb Hershelah," they said with a solemn voice, "the Rebbe said that he will leave the world today."

Reb Hershelah quickly dressed and rushed to his father's room. When he arrived at his father's side, Reb Hershelah started weeping, "Father, father, please don't leave us."

The Baal Shem Tov reached out and held his son's hand. "My dear son, I'm going to depart from this world. One thing I want you to know is that you have a very holy soul. When your mother and I conceived you, the very heavens shook. At that time, I had the power to bring any soul I chose, even that of Adam HaRishon. But I selected your soul because it was very holy and possessed all that you will need."

"Please father, tell me something before you depart," begged Reb Hershelah.

So the Baal Shem Tov started to speak to his son, but his voice was barely audible.

"Father, I can't understand what you are trying to tell me," said Reb Hershelah in a distraught voice.

The Baal Shem Tov gathered his strength and spoke louder, "My dearest son, there is nothing that I can do now. Just listen and remember this name."

Then the Baal Shem Tov motioned to his son to come closer. Reb Hershelah bent down very near to his father and the Baal Shem Tov whispered the name to him. Then he said, "Whenever you concentrate on this name, I will come and study with you."

Reb Hershelah spoke, "But what if I forget the name?"

"Come close to me again," said the Baal Shem Tov, "and I'll tell you a way of remembering the name."

After the Baal Shem Tov whispered the way to remember to Reb Hershelah, he closed his eyes and his soul ascended.

And to this day, no one knows the name or how to remember the name.

And so it was.

APPENDIX

GLOSSARY

Adam HaRishon — The first man.

Aliyah HaNeshama — Ascent of the Soul.

Ari HaKodesh — Arizal Rabbi Shlomo Itzhaki (1040-1105).

Avraham Avinu — The Patriarch Abraham our father.

Ayn Yaakov — A compilation of all the Aggadic material in the Talmud together with commentaries.

Baal Shem — Rabbi that utilized the powers of Kabbalah to heal the sick, ward off Demonic spirits and predict the future.

Baal Teshuvah — One who repents and returns to belief in G•d and the observance of the Mitzvos (Divine Commandment).

Baruch Hashem — Thank G•d.

Bat Mitzvah — Jewish girl reaches the age of maturity (12 years old) when she is responsible for her actions.

Beis Din — Jewish court.

Beis Hamikdosh — The Holy Temple.

Benching — Saying the Grace after meals.

Besht — Acronym for Baal Shem Tov.

Birchas Kohanim — Priestly blessing.

Bris — Circumcision.

Challah — Braided bread eaten on Shabbos and festivals.

Chosson — The groom.

Chasana — A wedding.

Chassidus — Mystical explanations of the Torah.

Chazzan — Leader of communal prayer.

Cheder — Hebrew day school for young boys.

Chaburah — Group of friends.

Chavrayah Kaddisha — Group of Holy friends.

Chupah — A wedding canopy.

GLOSSARY

Chumash — Five books of Moses.

Darshan — One who expounds on the Midrashic teachings of the Torah.

Daven — Pray.

Dveikus — Cleaving to G•d.

Eliyahu HaNavi — Elijah the Prophet.

Festivals — Rosh HaShanah, Yom Kippur, Succos, Pesach, etc.

Gabbai — Custodian of the shule.

Gartle — A prayer belt worn by Chassidim.

Get — Bill of divorce.

Goan Olam — World class Torah scholar.

Ha Kodesh Boruch Hu — The Holy One Blessed be He.

HaMotzi — Prayer said over bread.

HaShem — The Name (G•d).

Havdalah — a ritual prayer recited at the close of Shabbos and other holy days that marks the separation between holy days and the ordinary days of the week.

Ilui — Genius.

Ineffable Name — 72 letter name of G•d.

Kabbalah — The teachings and doctrines that deal with the Jewish Mystical Tradition.

Kallah — A bride.

Kameya — An amulet.

Kashrus — Food in accord with Jewish law, termed kosher in English.

Kavanah — Intention or direction of the heart.

Kelipot — "Husk" in Kabbalistic thought, the aspect of evil or impurity that obscures the holy and good.

Kiddush — The ritual of sanctification of Shabbos or Yom Tov, usually recited over a cup of wine.

Klaf — Animal skin used for scrolls such as Mezuzahs, Tefillin, Sefer Torahs.

Kvittel — A note in which the petitioner writes out his or her request.

Maariv — The evening prayer service.

Machpelah — A cave in Hebron where Adam and Eve, Abraham and Sarah, Isaac and Rebecca, and Yaakov and Leah are buried.

Mashka — Liquor.

Matronita — The Shechinah — the female aspect of G•d.

Melavah Malkah — Meal eaten after the conclusion of the Shabbos that celebrates the return of the Shabbos Queen to heaven, where she dwells until the next Shabbos, when she returns once again.

Melamed — Hebrew teacher for young boys.

Mesirus nefesh — Great self sacrifice.

Mincha — The afternoon prayer service.

Minyan — Ten Jewish men needed for communal prayer.

Mitzvos — Divine commandments.

Mikveh — Pool for ritual immersion.

Mitzvah — Divine commandment.

Moshe Rabbeinu — Moses our teacher.

Moshiach — Messiah.

Neshamah — G•dly Soul.

Neshamah Chadasha — A new soul that had not previously occupied a physical body.

Niggun — Spiritual melody without words.

Parnassah — Money livelihood.

Posul — Not kosher.

Rasha — Wicked person.

Rashi — Rabbi Shlomo Itzhaki (1040-1105).

Reb — Title of respect like Mister, usually followed by the person's forename.

Rebbe — Spiritual master and leader of a Chassidic sect.

Rosh Chodesh — First day of Jewish month.

Rosh yeshiva — Dean of a yeshiva.

Satan — Angel that serves as the Adversary.

Sefer — Sacred Hebrew Book.

Segulah — An action that is reputed to lead to a change in one's fortunes.

Seudah — Meal.

GLOSSARY

Seudah Shlishit — The third meal, traditionally eaten on Shabbos before sunset.

Shabbos — Jewish for the Sabbath.

Shadchan — Matchmaker.

Shalom Aleichem — Peace be to you.

Shamash — Synagogue caretaker.

Shechinah — The female aspect of G•d.

Shochet — A Jewish slaughterer that kills the animals in accordance with the requirements of Jewish law.

Shule — Synagogue.

Siddur — The book of daily ritual Hebrew prayers.

Simcha — Joyous celebration.

Shtetl — Small town.

Tallis — Prayer shawl.

Tannaim — Jewish Sages of the Mishnah 10 CE — 220CE.

Tefillin — Also called phylacteries are two small cubic leather boxes painted black, containing scrolls of parchment inscribed with verses from the

Torah, strapped to head and arm with black leather straps typically worn by Jewish men during weekday morning prayers.

Tehillim — Psalms.

Teshuvah — Repentance; literally turning back to G•d.

Tikunei Zohar — A book of Kabbalah.

Tish — Literally a table in Jewish. Among Chassidim, a tish refers to any joyous public celebration or gathering or meal by Chassidim at a "table" of their Rebbe.

Torah — Twenty Four canonized scriptures of traditional Judaism. It consists of the Five Books of Moses, the Prophets, and the Writings. The Torah can also mean any spiritual text book or idea that is connected to traditional Judaism.

Treife — Non-kosher.

Tzaddik — Holy man.

Tzaddik nistar — a hidden holy man.

Tzedeka — Charity.

Upscherinish — The first cutting of a boys hair at three years old.

Yetzer Hara — Evil Inclination.

Yechudim — "Yichudim" are a form of kabalistic meditation based on different permutations and combinations of the Divine Names and attributes of G•d.

Yechidus — Private audience with a Rebbe.

Zaida — Grandfather in Yiddish.

BIBLIOGRAPHY

1. BAAL SHEM TOV GENESIS Vol. I by Tzvi Meir Cohn

2. BAAL SHEM TOV EXODUS Vol. II by Tzvi Meir Cohn

3. BAAL SHEM TOV LEVITICUS Vol. III by Tzvi Meir Cohn

4. BAAL SHEM TOV NUMBERS Vol. V by Tzvi Meir Cohn

5. BAAL SHEM TOV HOLY DAYS Vol. VI by Tzvi Meir Cohn

6. BAAL SHEM TOV FAITH LOVE AND JOY Vol. I by Tzvi Meir Cohn

7. BAAL SHEM TOV DIVINE LIGHT Vol. II by Tzvi Meir Cohn

8. BAAL SHEM TOV HEART OF PRAYER Vol. III by Tzvi Meir Cohn

9. IN PRAISE OF THE BAAL SHEM TOV Translated and edited by Dan Ben-Amos and Jerome R. Mintz

10. STORIES OF THE BAAL SHEM TOV by Rabbi Yisrael Yaakov Klapholtz

11. A TREASURY OF CHASSIDIC TALES ON THE
    FESTIVALS
    by Rabbi Shlomo Yoseph Zevin
12. A TREASURY OF CHASSIDIC TALES ON THE
    TORAH
    by Rabbi Shlomo Yoseph Zevin
13. SEEKER OF SLUMBERING SOULS
    by Rabbi Zalman Ruderman
14. THE PATH OF THE BAAL SHEM TOV
    by Rabbi David Sears
15. ESSENTIAL PAPERS ON CHASSIDISM
    Edited by Gershon David Hundert
16. MEETINGS WITH REMARKABLE SOULS
    by Rabbi Eliyahu Klein
17. CLASSIC CHASSIDIC TALES
    by Meyer Levin
18. STORY TELLING AND SPIRITUALITY IN
    JUDAISM
    by Maggid Yitzhak Buxbaum
19. THE LIGHT BEYOND
    by Rabbi Aryeh Kaplan
20. TZAVA'AT HARIVASH
    by Rabbi Jacob Immanuel Shochet
21. THE LIGHT AND FIRE OF THE BAAL SHEM
    TOV
    by Maggid Yitzhak Buxbaum

22. THE BESHT
   by Professor Emanuel Etkes
23. EXTRAORDINARY CHASSIDIC TALES
   by Rabbi Rafael Nachman Kahn
24. THE GREAT MISSION
   by Rabbi Eli Friedman
25. CHASSIDIC MASTERS
   by Rabbi Aryeh Kaplan
26. THE RELIGIOUS THOUGHT OF CHASSIDIM
   by Rabbi Norman Lamm
27. HASIDIC TALES
   by Rabbi Rami Shapiro

SOURCES OF THE
BAAL SHEM TOV STORIES

Chapter One [DEVARIM]
A SPEEDY JOURNEY

Freely adapted by Tzvi Meir Cohane Cohn from a story found in SHIVCHEI HABESHT as translated in STORIES OF THE BAAL SHEM TOV by Y.Y. Klapholtz.

THE MAGIC MIRROR

Freely adapted by Tzvi Meir HaCohane Cohn from a story found in SIPUREI CHASSIDIM and translated in STORIES OF THE BAAL SHEM TOV by Y.Y. Klapholtz.

Chapter Two [VA'ESCHANAN]
THE DEFECTIVE MEZUZAH

Freely adapted by Tzvi Meir HaCohane Cohn from a story found in SHIVCHEI HABESHT and translated in IN PRAISE OF THE BAAL SHEM TOV by Ben Amos and Mintz.

THE BOOK

Freely adapted by Tzvi Meir HaCohane Cohn from a story found in STORIES OF THE BAAL SHEM TOV by Y.Y. Klapholtz.

THE LIGHT AND FIRE OF THE BAAL SHEM TOV by Maggid Yitzhak Buxbaum.

SHIVCHEI HABESHT and translated in IN PRAISE OF THE BAAL SHEM TOV by Ben Amos and Mintz.

Chapter Three [EIKEV]
A BUNDLE OF GREENS

Freely adapted by Tzvi Meir HaCohane Cohn from a story published by Rabbi Yerachmiel Tilles of Ascent in Safed, Israel

THE MAGICAL POWER OF TEFILLIN

Freely adapted by Tzvi Meir HaCohane Cohn from a story found in SHIVCHEI HABESHT and translated in IN PRAISE OF THE BAAL SHEM TOV by Ben Amos and Mintz.

Chapter Four [RE'EH]
THE UNTRUSTWORTHY SHOCHET

Freely adapted by Tzvi Meir HaCohane Cohn from a story found in SHIVCHEI HABESHT and translated in IN PRAISE OF THE BAAL SHEM TOV by Ben Amos and Mintz.

THE EXTINGUISHED WESTERN LIGHT

Freely adapted by Tzvi Meir HaCohane Cohn from a story in GEVUROS ARI and translated in STORIES OF THE BAAL SHEM TOV by Y. Y. Klapholtz.

Chapter Five [SHOFTIM]
FALSE TESTIMONY

Freely adapted by Tzvi Meir HaCohane Cohn from a story in SIPUREI YAAKOV as translated in STORIES OF THE BAAL SHEM TOV by Y.Y. Klapholtz.

A JEWISH KING

Freely adapted by Tzvi Meir HaCohane Cohn from a story found in DIVREI TZADDIKIM and translated in STORIES OF THE BAAL SHEM TOV by Y.Y. Klapholtz.

CHAPTER SIX [KI SEITZEI]
REB MICHEL'S KAMEYA

Freely adapted by Tzvi Meir HaCohane Cohn from a story found in DEVORIM AREIVIM and translated in STORIES OF THE BAAL SHEM TOV by Y.Y. Klapholtz.

THE STRENGTH OF THE TZADDIK'S WORDS

Freely adapted by Tzvi Meir HaCohane Cohn from a story found in A TREASURY OF CHASSIDIC TALES by Rabbi S.Y. Zevin.

Chapter Seven [KI SAVO]
THE BAAL SHEM TOV AND THE BIRTH OF SCHNEUR ZALMAN

Freely adapted by Tzvi Meir HaCohane Cohn from a story found in SEFER HATOLDOS.

THE TRANSFERENCE

Freely adapted by Tzvi Meir HaCohane Cohn from a story found in SHIVCHEI HABESHT and translated in IN PRAISE OF THE BAAL SHEM TOV by Ben Amos and Mintz.

Chapter Eight [NITZAVIM]
THE ZOLOTCHOVER WATER CARRIER

Freely adapted by Tzvi Meir HaCohane Cohn from a story found in SIPUREI CHASSIDIM and translated in STORIES OF THE BAAL SHEM TOV by Y.Y. Klapholtz.

IMPERFECT TRUTH AND PERFECT FAITH

Freely adapted by Tzvi Meir HaCohane Cohn from a story in A TREASURY OF CHASSIDIC TALES by Rabbi S.Y. Zevin.

Chapter Nine [VAYEILECH]
THE PASSING

Freely adapted by Tzvi Meir HaCohane Cohn from a story found in SHIVCHEI HABESHT and translated in IN PRAISE OF THE BAAL SHEM TOV by Ben Amos and Mintz.

FEIVISH LOWEST OF THE LOW

Freely adapted by Tzvi Meir HaCohane Cohn from a story recounted by Reb Kahana Nachman, the Spinker Rebbe, as reported in TALES OF THE BAAL SHEM TOV by Y.Y. Klapholtz.

Chapter Ten [HA'AZINU]

A NEW WAY OF SERVING

Freely adapted by Tzvi Meir HaCohane Cohn from a story found in BUTZINA DINEHORA as translated in STORIES OF THE BAAL SHEM TOV by Y.Y. Klapholtz.

THE HIDDEN TZADDIK

Freely adapted by Tzvi Meir HaCohane Cohn from a story found in the WRITINGS AND TALKS of Rabbi Yosef Yitzchak Schneersohn, the sixth Rebbe of Chabad.

Chapter Eleven [VEZOS HABRACHAH]
THE NIGGUN OF AROUSAL

Freely adapted by Tzvi Meir HaCohane Cohn from a story found in STORIES OF THE BAAL SHEM TOV by Y.Y. Klapholtz.

THE LAST REVELATION

Freely adapted by Tzvi Meir HaCohane Cohn from a story found in SHIVCHEI HABESHT and translated in IN PRAISE OF THE BAAL SHEM TOV by Ben Amos and Mintz.

The following is the original from Igros Kodesh Vol.
6 written by the Previous Rebbe[i]

וכחמעשה חידוע:

תוד כ״ק אאזמו״ר חרה״ק צמח צדק זצוקללה״ח נבג״מ זי״ע הואיל
לשלוח את הרב הגאון האמיתי החסיד הנודע מוח״ר יצחק אייזיק נ״ע
הלוי עפשטיין מהאמליע לכ״ק אדמו״ר מוה״ר ישראל מרוזין
זצוקללה״ח נבג״מ זי״ע בהנוגע לענין הכלל.

החסיד הר״א להיותו מחניכי חסידי חב״ד התענין במאד לדעת את
ארחות והנהגות חסידי רוזין בכלל והנהגותיו של כ״ק ר׳ ישראל מרוזין
בפרט וישם דעתו הרחבה ולבו על כל דבר הנהגה בפרט.

הסדר אצל כ״ק ר׳ ישראל מרוזין הי׳ אשר בעת קבלת שלום –
הנהוג אצל חסידי פולין ואהלין – וכן בשעת קבלת אנשים – פראווע׳ן
זיך – וקריאת הפתקאות – קוויטלעך – חנה המקורב – אחד מיחידי
סגולה מזקני החסידים אשר בחר בו כ״ק ר׳ ישראל להיות המתורגמן
בינו ובין החסידים והי׳ מכונה בשם מקורב – הי׳ עומד על ימינו וגבאי
הראשון משמאלו.

בין האורחים שהיו אז ברוזין הי׳ אחד מגדולי הרבנים בבוקאווינא
מפורסם ללמדן גדול וממקושריו הכי גדולים של כ״ק ר׳ ישראל והביא
את חבורו לקבל עליו הסכמתו של כ״ק ר׳ ישראל, וגם אחד החסידים
בא אשר אסף כמה שנים ספורי מעשיות מצדיקים וחסידים ויביא גם
הוא את חבורו לקחת הסכמת מכ״ק ר׳ ישראל.

בשעת קבלת האנשים עמדו שני החסידים המקושרים חנ״ל, הרב
והחסיד, וחבוריהם בידיהם. המקורב – ע״פ הוראת כ״ק ר׳ ישראל –
לקח את ספריהם מידיהם ויקרא לפני כ״ק ר׳ ישראל איזה מקומות
מחבורו של הרב ואח״כ קרא איזה ספורים מספרו של החסיד המלקט.

כ״ק ר׳ ישראל ישב בדבקות ואח״כ תתחיל לדבר בדבר מעלת
ספורי צדיקים והרושם הגדול שדבר זה עושה בהיכלי הצדיקים בגן
עדן, ואח״כ דיבר בעניני חדושי תורה באותם הענינים אשר המקורב
קרא לפניו מספרו של הרב בפלפול רב, ואח״כ צוה להמקורב לכתוב
את הסכמתו על שני הספרים.

החסיד התחב״די הרי״א נ״ע הסתכל בתשומת לב על הסדר בקבלת
האנשים ועל יחס כ״ק ר׳ ישראל למקושריו ויתפלא על עומק הפלפול
וסגנונו שחידש כ״ק ר׳ ישראל בחדושי התורה של הרב, אבל הי׳
מוקשה לו מדוע הקדים כ״ק ר׳ ישראל את הערותיו וכן את הצווי
לכתוב את הסכמתו לספר הלקוטים של ספורי המעשיות להערותיו

182

SOURCES OF THE BAAL SHEM TOV STORIES

על חדושי תורה של הרב וצוויו לכתוב הסכמה על ספרו. ויהי לפלא
בעיניו.

כיומים אחרי כן הי' ראש חדש, והחסיד חרי"א הזמן לסעודת
ראש חדש ובתוך הסעודה אמר כ"ק ר' ישראל דברי תורה וקודם ברכת
המזון אמר: ביים ליטווישען גאון איז געווען א פלא אויף אונז וואס
מיר האבען גערעט וועגען די ספורי צדיקים און ערשט דערנאך וועגען
די חדושי תורה און וואס מיר האבען געגעבן אונזער הסכמה פריער
אויף דעם חיבור פון די ספורי צדיקים און דערנאך אויף דעם חבור פון
חדושי תורה.

דאס איז באמת א גרויסע און איין אלטע קשיא וואס רש"י הקדוש
ועלכער איז געווען א גאון ועולם אין נגלה און אין נסתר פרעגט די
זעלבע קשיא אין דעם ערשטען פסוק בראשית לא הי' צריך להתחיל
את התורה אלא מהחדש הזה לכם ומה טעם פתח בבראשית משום כח
מעשיו הגיד, די נשמה וואס אין די מעשים וואס אין דער בריאה בכל
עת ובכל רגע.

דער זיידעניו, דער חייליגער גרויסער מגיד האט מקבל געווען פון
דעם חייליגען בעש"ט א דרך ווי צו זעהן אין יעדער זאך די נשמה
ועלכע איז אין דעם גוף פון דער זאך.

איר פארשטייט – פנח כ"ק ר' ישראל מרוזין אל החסיד חרי"א –
מיר גייען מיט דעם סדר ווי חשי"ת האט געגעבן אונז די חייליגער תורה
פריער ספר בראשית – ספורי צדיקים, ווי דער מדרש זאגט זאבט במי נמלך
בנשמותיהן של צדיקים און נאכדעם ספר שמות – החדש הזה לכם.

ביידע מחברים זיינען חסידים בעלי צורה, ביידע חבורים זיינען
חדושים נפלאים, די חדושי תורה דערציילן די גרויסע לומדות און
סברות וואס דער מחבר האט מחדש געווען אין דער חייליגער תורה
און די ספורי צדיקים דערציילן די גרויסע חדושים וואס חשי"ת האט
מחדש געווען און איז מחדש אין דער וועלט, דערום האבן מיר מקדים
געווען די הסכמה אויף דעם ספר ספורי צדיקים פאר דער הסכמה
אויף דעם ספר חדשי תורה.

ספור זה אינו דורש ביאור כי מבואר חוא באר היטב באלפי אותות
מחיי יום יום גם במפלגת החסידים עצמם – לא רק במעלת החסידים
על שאינם חסידים אלא גם בין החסידים בעצמם – במעלת בעלי
העבודה על בעלי השכלה.

---

[i]Rabbi Yosef Yitzchak Schneerson [1880-1950] the sixth
Rebbe of Chabad-Lubavitch

WWW.MEZUZAH.NET

Home of the World Wide Mezuzah Campaign

The fundamental goal of The World Wide Mezuzah Campaign is to unify the Jewish people. By fulfilling the mitzvah of Mezuzah, this unity can be accomplished by each Jewish person: man, woman or child. The mitzvah can be easily fulfilled by affixing a Mezuzah on the "Doorpost of Your House or upon Your Gates," as required by Jewish law.

Purchase Mezuzahs written in Israel by a Certified Scribe, then checked by a computer for accuracy and finally checked by a second Certified Scribe before we send it to you. Our Mezuzahs are of a very high quality, and they are beautifully written. They are shipped to you in a Mezuzah case ready to mount on your door.

www.mezuzah.net
The World Wide Mezuzah Campaign.
A project of the Baal Shem Tov Foundation
a 501(c) (3), non-profit organization

Baal Shem Tov Times

Spreading the light of the legendary
Kabbalah Master and Mystic
Rabbi Yisrael Baal Shem Tov

-A weekly email publication-

Regular Features:

Baal Shem Tov Story
Torah Baal Shem Tov
Heart of Prayer
Divine Light
Kesser Shem Tov

Subscribe to receive your FREE weekly
e-mail edition at
www.baalshemtov.com

ABOUT THE AUTHOR

Tzvi Meir (Howard M.) Cohn is a Patent and Trademark Attorney (www.CohnPatents.com). He attended Yeshiva Hadar Hatorah in Crown Heights, Brooklyn after completing his university studies in Engineering and Law. While studying at the Yeshiva, he discovered a deep connection to the stories and teachings of the Baal Shem Tov. More recently, he founded the Baal Shem Tov Foundation which is dedicated to spreading the teachings of the Baal Shem Tov throughout the world in order to hasten the coming of the Moshiach. To spread the teachings of the Baal Shem Tov, Tzvi Meir created a website, www.BaalShemTov.com and publishes a weekly newsletter, the Baal Shem Tov Times. Also, Tzvi Meir initiated the World Wide Mezuzah Campaign (www.Mezuzah.net) as a project of the Baal Shem Tov Foundation. Tzvi Meir gives live presentations of his original music and Baal Shem Tov stories to welcoming audiences.

OTHER BOOKS BY

TZVI MEIR HACOHANE COHN

BAAL SHEM TOV FAITH LOVE AND JOY Vol. I

BAAL SHEM TOV DIVINE LIGHT Vol. II

BAAL SHEM TOV HEART OF PRAYER Vol. III

BAAL SHEM TOV GENESIS Vol. I

BAAL SHEM TOV EXODUS Vol. II

BAAL SHEM TOV LEVITICUS Vol. III

BAAL SHEM TOV NUMBERS Vol. IV

BAAL SHEM TOV HOLY DAYS Vol. VI

Made in the USA
Columbia, SC
01 February 2021